AFFLUENCE
~ AND ~
# DISCONTENT

AFFLUENCE
~ AND ~
DISCONTENT

The Anatomy of Consumer Societies

Eugene Linden

A SEAVER BOOK
THE VIKING PRESS   NEW YORK

For Madelaine

Copyright © Eugene Linden, 1979
All rights reserved

A Seaver Book/The Viking Press
First published in 1979 by The Viking Press
625 Madison Avenue, New York, N.Y. 10022

Published simultaneously in Canada by
Penguin Books Canada Limited

LIBRARY OF CONGRESS CATALOGING IN PUBLICATION DATA
Linden, Eugene.
Affluence and discontent.
"A Seaver book."
1. Consumers. 2. Civilization, Modern—20th
century. I. Title.
HC79.c6L56   301.2   79–13207
ISBN 0–670–23943–7

Printed in the United States of America
Set in Linotron Primer

ACKNOWLEDGMENTS

I owe a great debt to Kenneth Cavander, whose lectures on the functions and nature of myth inspired me to develop the thoughts presented in this book. At a time when I was trying to develop a perspective on modern behavior that had no home in any formal discipline, Kenneth Cavander encouraged me to pursue my theories. Over the past ten years I have benefited as well from the insights of a number of scholars in different fields. Many of these people are mentioned in the course of this book. One ongoing dialogue that has been particularly helpful has been with Leon Levy, who has considerably brightened my understanding of the elusive world of markets. Finally, I would like to thank Iver Kern for his thoughtful critique of my manuscript, and I would like to thank my father-in-law, Brendan Gill, whose critical guidance has saved me from a number of stylistic misadventures.

Contents

Introduction:
A Protean Juggernaut

Discontent in the West has traditionally been interpreted as an indication of the basic instability of modern materialistic societies and a signal of imminent decline. However, a broad look at consumer societies leads to the conclusion that individual discontents and their larger manifestation in countercultural movements are actually a necessary part of a consumer society. Such expressions of mass discontent, far from being an indication of decline, are the way a consumer society brings new areas of behavior within its ambit.

This book is about the evolutionary forces that have produced the need to sell and the need to buy that we attribute to consumer societies. It will try to show that consumer behavior is much more encompassing than the mere buying and selling of consumer goods. It will try to show that a profound and ancient conflict in our evolution has produced these needs and that these needs are part of a protean personality—the consumer personality. The hallmark of the consumer is his extreme flexibility. Like Proteus, the consumer can adapt to any environment, and, like Proteus, for all these changes of form, the substance of the consumer remains the same. This is the tragic irony of the consumer society: it is so well equipped to assimilate change without changing itself that it has lost a critically important faculty of all cultures, that is, to recognize and adapt to true danger. Thus, for all its flexibility, the consumer society is a juggernaut, hurtling toward a confrontation with its own contradictions. This book attempts to show where consumer societies came from, what they really are, and what the nature of consumer behavior suggests about their destiny. To start with we have to step outside our accustomed ways of looking at modern societies.

In the early 1900s, ethologist Eugene Marais came to the conclusion that the "soul" of the white ant lay not in the individual ant, but in the ant colony. The functions of the individual ants are so specialized that no ant might survive on its own, and the organization of the ant colony is such that many ants perform suicidal functions that insure the survival of the colony. Clearly, then, the adaptive unit in the case of the white ant is the colony rather than the individual ant. The colony is the organism, and its needs rule the adaptations of individual ants. More recently this argument has been applied to animal societies, and more recently still, to human cultures. Anthropologists have written about the ways in which different primitive and non-Western cultures "trick" their members into performing roles essential to the survival of the society, although such actions are not always in the self-interest of the individual. As in the case of the ant colony, the *culture* operates as an adaptive unit, adjusting the behavior of the individual to the rigors of the tribe's environmental situation.*
This book will argue that the above model of the relationship between the individual, his society, and his environment also applies to modern consumer societies. And so, right off, I should say that although I will continue to use the familiar term consumer society, this book will argue that the more comprehensive term culture should be used to characterize consumer behavior.

That modern man is not exempt from the organizing principles of nature should not surprise. This approach can explain modern consumer behavior with a diminished concept of human autonomy. However, whatever pricks to our pride this approach might force us to endure, it also allows us to understand where consumer societies come from, how they figure in the evolutionary scheme of things, in what funda-

---

*By culture I am referring to a group of people united by commonly shared beliefs and customs.

mental ways they contrast with nonconsumer societies, and how all the various aspects of consumer societies cohere to achieve the purposes of the consumer "colony." In short, the search for correlations between that mysterious "soul" of the white ant and the "soul" of a modern consumer society yields a productive, and, as we shall see, somewhat startling theory of behavior.

Crucial to any theory that attempts to characterize the nature of a culture is a credible description of the devices that relate individual actions to the total behavior of the group. Such a problem is compounded when the group in question has, as ours does, so deep a stake in the notion of self-determination. We are not particularly receptive to hearing that we are pawns in a game that is not of our devising. This is precisely the point that this book will attempt to make. In doing so I will also try to show how some of the enduring myths of consumer societies comfort and "trick" us in just the same manner that the myths of primitive societies "trick" a tribe into proper tribal behavior. With regard to consumer societies this crucial relationship between the individual and the group is explained by the consumer personality, a commonly shared set of appetites and needs that organize individual activities in accord with the needs of consumer culture as a whole. It will be a major task of this book to argue the existence of such a personality, and then to demonstrate the particular ways in which this personality serves the larger purpose of a consumer society.

The term consumer personality is ripe for misunderstanding. It does not refer to a superficial set of material appetites foisted on an innocent public by a sinister corporate elite. The relationship between our corporate superstructure and the material appetites it coaxes and services involves much more complex interrelationships than an economic conspiracy theory might encompass. Nor is the consumer personality merely the hat a person wears when he or she goes shopping. Rather, I will try to argue, the consumer personality is a way of looking at the world that conditions every aspect of daily life, and that it is not something that can be abandoned simply because someone no longer wants to be a consumer. The consumer personality *is* founded upon a set of relationships, gradually assembled during the course of Western history, which translates religious needs into material appetites. Ultimately, the consumer personality is rooted in an unresolved conflict between man's rational and irrational selves, a conflict that is the most ancient problem of human nature. Thus, another task of this book will be to show how consumer behavior grew out of nonconsumer behavior, and also to discuss the specific historical and evolutionary events that contributed to the advent of a consumer culture. Even if one accepts the existence of the consumer personality, there is still the question of how the consumer culture selects and organizes *proper* consumer behavior through that personality. The answer to this question yields the most startling insights into the hidden purposes of the economic, cultural, and political organization of the United States, the place where the artifice I call consumer behavior was finally completed. Understood in its historical perspective, consumer behavior is a device to further the "rational" management of human behavior and our environment. What consumer behavior does, essentially, is extend rational control over behaviors and areas of the environment previously managed by tradition, in the case of behavior, or nature, in the case of the environment. How it does this is the genius of consumer culture.

One of the broadest patterns of Western history has been a trend toward the gradual diminution of the influence of religion and tradition as a force in daily life as "reason" has more and more made itself felt in all aspects of life. Religion has not only diminished in authority, but the religions themselves have until recently become increasingly desiccated and rationalistic. This has created a reservoir of disenfranchised religious needs that can find no normal expression in modern life. Not to force a pun, but these disenfranchised religious contents form the working capital of a consumer society. Reason's stranglehold on behavior first produces a congestion of disenfranchised needs, and then these needs are translated through the genius of the consumer personality into a set of material appetites, the satisfaction of which further extends reason's hegemony. Thus the Gods are captured and put to work in the service of reason. The precise ways in which these needs are translated into material appetites will be the subject of later chapters. The net effect, however, is that a potentially disruptive force is harnessed as a source of power for the very culture that repressed the needs originally. Thus we have the paradox of a society that is fueled by the very dissatisfactions it creates. This is a useful piece of knowledge, if one is to understand some of the "problems" that cyclically afflict consumer societies.

The recurrent outlaw cultural movements that seem to plague consumer societies have been persistently misunderstood as threats. I will try to show that, on the contrary, countercultural movements are a sign that the consumer mechanism is in fine working order. These large cultural spasms are merely macrocosmic examples of the basic manner in which the consumer culture creates dissatisfactions and then domesticates this outlaw energy. It is a syndrome that characterizes the myriad individual purchases that invigorate the consumer society. Our society depends on alienation for its very life.

Actually many of the endemic problems of modern life take on new meaning when understood in terms of the complex forces that motivate consumer societies. Crime, pollution, inflation, and a host of other persistent problems are bound up with the basic engines of consumer societies. I will try to show that certain problems persist because they cannot be solved without endangering the "health" of the consumer society, and I will try to show how efforts to solve some of these endemic problems really act not to solve problems but instead act to divert this reformist energy in harmless ways and thus abate the anxiety that problems persist that are not being solved.

The purpose of this book then is to offer a novel view of behavior. It will show how consumer behavior fits within the scheme of evolution and history, and in so doing it will offer a theory of consumer societies which, it is hoped, will both illuminate the purposes of many of the commonplace phenomena we associate with consumer behavior, as well as bring under one roof our understanding of the complexities of modern life. This book poses the hypothesis that a modern consumer society behaves like an organism, and that, as an organism, the roles filled by the individuals that comprise the society are selected by the needs of the organism. The book will also hypothesize that the device that binds the individual to the needs of the consumer society as a whole is a commonly shared configuration of personality which for convenience is called the consumer personality. The consumer personality develops during childhood and is manifest in the way the consumer analyzes and relates to the world around him. It is a type of deep structure conditioning, not just economic behavior, but political and cultural behavior as well. Our access to this consumer personality is through the consumer decisions or "purchases" the individual makes in these various modalities, and the argument for the existence of this personality rests on communalities that relate these various kinds of consumer decisions.

Perhaps then it would be best to commence this undertaking by looking at a consumer decision and the characteristics of this purchase that spurred the development of the following theory of consumer behavior.

~ PART I ~
Curiosities

Part I presents a series of curious phenomena:
1. Buyers who are in effect possessed at the moment they make critical consumer decisions.
2. Expatriates who try to flee the consumer society only to discover that it is a state of mind, as is the paradise they seek.
3. Avid consumers who demonstrate that consumer behavior is not just a question of buying consumer goods.

~1~

The Consumer Decision

THE SALESMAN / POLITICIAN

One of the curiosities of modern life is our inexhaustible capacity to be taken in by people who have been certified as crooks. Voters regularly return to office politicians who have been indicted or even convicted of crimes. Sophisticated investors regularly are fleeced by promoters with known criminal records pushing tax shelters or franchising operations that would not survive the most cursory investigation. Ordinary people, with a canny eye for bargains at the supermarket, regularly commit large sums to purchase items peddled door-to-door that they had not even considered buying before the salesman showed up. During all these consumer decisions—voting, investing, purchasing—something seems to suspend the common sense and caution of normally astute people, something that also surrounds the crooked politician, promoter, or salesman with an aura of honesty and power. This chapter will consider my discovery of the nature of that "something" and its role in American life.

Huey Long, George Wallace, Fidel Castro, and Billy Graham all have two things in common. Each has commanded a large mass following, and each has been, at some point early in his career, a door-to-door salesman. Unlikely bedfellows such as Nikita Khrushchev and Lyndon Johnson were also in sales at some point in their lives. The transition from door-to-door hustler to politician is an American archetype. In one of the

3

bewildering transformations of American life, individuals from a profession accorded almost universal scorn are regularly catapulted into positions of the highest trust. Nowhere was this enigma more engrossing than in the case of Richard Nixon, whose admirers chuckled over his likeness to that paradigm of venality—the used-car salesman—as he was elected president by one of the greatest majorities in American history. Moreover, it is not as though salesmen undergo some apotheosis when they reemerge as politicians, for in the public esteem, politicians rank just below slave traders. Rather, there is an unresolved contradiction in American attitudes towards both salesmen and politicians: we talk about them with great skepticism, and yet, over and over again, we buy their products.

Our collective impression of salesmen is best summarized by the traveling-salesman joke. The elements are always the same—corrupt salesman screws somebody, he gets caught, but *he* has the last laugh (even if on his friend). In the collective mind of the country, salesmen screw people; nobody ever got a good deal from a salesman, and yet everyone has bought something from a salesman, and everyone swears he got a good deal.

The reason we preserve this infinite capacity to be fooled has to do with the special nature of the relationship between the buyer and the salesman. Although the same person might disparage salesmen and politicians as thieves and knaves and then later patronize the worst examples of each, the disparager and patron are actually two different people. The frustrations of dealing with salesmen and politicians is that both tap a part of the consumer's personality that the consumer himself does not have access to. I made this discovery during a stint as a cold-canvass encyclopedia salesman.

THE COLD-CANVASS SALESMAN

I stumbled into this job in 1968 during the summer after my junior year in college. I was looking for a way to pay for my senior year. After striking out with salmon trawlers in Seattle, I looked at a San Francisco paper. In the want-ad section was an ad that might have been written by the supreme tempter himself. The gist of the ad was that a publisher was looking for college students as editorial trainees and was willing to pay qualified applicants $135 a week. Taking that ad seriously required a naiveté on the order of Jeff Bridges's in *Hearts of the West*, when he packed his bags to visit the "campus" of his correspondence school, but I was on the next plane south. The first meeting for applicants was packed with about two hundred other optimistic people, mostly students. Keep in mind that this was the summer of 1968 in San Francisco, the summer in which students were hypersensitive to the corruption and hypocrisy of the business world. Consequently, when it became clear that we were being recruited for door-to-door encyclopedia sales, about fifteen applicants walked out in disgust. The remaining 185 of us discreetly hid our morals while we waited for the other shoe to drop—namely, whether or not that $135-a-week salary was for real. It was not, of course, and *that* was when about one hundred more children of the new age stormed out in indignation.

I had flown in from Seattle for this job, and so with little alternative except to return East in failure, I decided to see it through. I must say that rarely has a business organization been more out of touch with its sales force than the shady managers of the New Standard Encyclopedia Company were with their sulky recruits. We were given a short course in door-to-door sales before being split into teams and sent out into the field. During that course, the eighty-five recruits dwindled to about fifty, with the bulk of the defections coming shortly after a trainer tried to lead us in the cheer, "Let's hear it for money." Although they did not want to cheer for money, it was its promise that kept the remaining trainees in the fold. However, this group of diehards was halved again when we began making the rounds door-to-door. Some left because, faced with the prospect of pitching a set of books they had never seen but rightly suspected were a sham, their moral instincts finally surfaced. Most left, though, because it was simply too difficult to sell the wretched books. Of the original group that underwent training, perhaps ten of us ever sold any encyclopedias, and perhaps five of us ever sold them regularly. Three of us were successful at it. I was successful simply because I listened to what these antediluvian entrepreneurs were saying, and because I followed their instructions and the sales pitch to the letter.

The characters who had put together the New Standard Encyclopedia Company were a group of former salesmen. They hailed from Atlanta. They had given their company the same name as a giant skyscraper in Atlanta. Their literature showed the company headquarters as this building. In fact, their only space in their "headquarters" was a mail drop. In the era of free love and the gates of perception, these former salesmen wore black shiny suits and acetate ties. They drank bourbon and supported the war. The trainees, flushed with their liberal arts educations and ideas of relevance, thought they were better equipped to reach Bay Area buyers. They would "rap" with the buyers, attempt to persuade. They regarded the sales pitch with scorn because of its lies and its cheap appeals to greed. They should have known better. The sales pitch was magic. Once during a training session, Richard Stryker, the company president, addressed the problem this way, "All of you who think you are being nice to those people in the field are just being weak. You want to be friends with them, right? Well, you go in and chat, and then I'll go in, sell 'em a set, take five hundred bucks from 'em and then we'll see who they choose for a friend, you or me!" Stryker was right, but his statement also lends insight into the motivations of a successful salesman.

Successful book salesmen can make a great deal of money, but I have noticed that often they do not spend lavishly and that they are casual about the luxuries they have acquired. When they are not in the field this tough genre of salesmen may be vulnerable and insecure, but on the job they are purely cunning and implacable (a quality of mind called a Positive Mental Attitude). These are the men from whom each of us has gotten a good deal. Ask them why they sell and often they will say something about the hours, that they have no boss, or that the money is good, or that they are not chained to a desk. But when I asked one salesman, Mohun Singh, if he sold for the money, he said no directly, and then said that were he in sales for the money, he would be nowhere. However, I could never pin Singh down to exactly why he did sell books. I suspect it was for the same reason most salesmen sell: the thrill of power, a masculine connection to the world, ratified through the sale.

THE SALES PERSONALITY

Singh is a cold-canvas encyclopedia salesman. He is a sleek Indian aristocrat who has been disinherited. Prohibited from further institutionalized preying on the lower castes and a failure as a student, Singh came here and began to prey off Americans of the middle castes, using only his wits. He draws from a vast vocabulary of facial expressions, voice colorations, and emotions; and he uses himself as an aeolian harp which plays according to the winds of the buyer's mood. There is a fullness to Singh's sales personality. Often a salesman will seem fishy, but Singh is not fishy in the least. He will gambol with some horrible little brat with such exuberance that even the kid will be fooled and think that Singh likes him.

During a pitch, Singh is at once as unobtrusive as a friendly uncle, and yet so obtrusive that customers grow furious at their inability to dislodge him from their homes. He leaves no edges to grab; he is undefinable and yet impossible to ignore. There is no lie he will not tell, and yet he is always indisputably Singh, and he is authentic.

Although Singh would not say why he sold, I could sense the satisfactions he derived from his manipulations. In an effective sales pitch, the salesman has such control that the customer is unaware that he is being manipulated and often thinks that he is using the salesman (although there may be some uneasiness in the back of his mind). Singh could be despicably slavish before a customer, but later he would contemptuously say, "I got the sale." The salesman ratifies his identity through the sale, and, as we shall see, the buyer preserves his identity through the purchase. It was my discovery that considerations of price and practicality were of residual importance in such transactions.

Since I sold encyclopedias in 1968, the personal techniques we were taught as useful in door-to-door sales have been pitched by various authors and gurus as the roads to success, power, and even self-awareness. We were taught how to use the handshake and introduction as a means of establishing authority and a way of preparing the "mooch" (buyer) for the pitch. We observed the erosive powers of an implacable recitation of the pitch on the buyer's resistance, we learned how to manipulate a husband and wife so that they conquer each other's doubts, how to position ourselves so that the buyers unconsciously accepted our authority in their house. And we were taught a host of other subtle tricks. It is interesting that these devices, which we employed with mounting self-disgust as the weeks wore on, are now promoted by the Robert Ringers, the Michael Kordas, and the Werner Erhards as the basis of a healthy personality. If nothing else, the similarities between door-to-door techniques and these self-awareness movements suggests the breadth of the "sales interaction" in American life. For me, the cruel tactics I used in pursuit of the sales were utterly detached from my personality. It was a role I assumed which lent effectiveness to the pitch I delivered. But once again my red-neck instructors were right: the tricks of sales, however coldly employed, worked, and indeed the salesman at his most rapacious had a far closer relationship with the buyer than those who went door-to-door trying to "communicate" with the household. Still, the real magic was in the sales pitch.

The managers computed their sales expectations on the basis of the number of presentations without taking into account the charisma or genius of the salesman. An effective sales personality might get the salesman in the door, but once inside it is the pitch that sells books. We were told that to sell one set of encyclopedias an evening meant delivering between three and four full pitches, which in turn meant finding between eight and sixteen "qualified" families (husband and wife both home, evidence of children, and the possibility of getting through the door). Again they were right. Once I had mastered the delivery, I was selling four or five sets of books a week, and the relationship of sales to presentations was close to what the managers had predicted. Nor was this virgin territory. The Bay Area cities had been worked by encyclopedia companies for years, and we were regularly crossing tracks with sales teams from the competing companies.

THE PITCH

Each afternoon we would pile into Joe Thomas's Mercury and head out over the Golden Gate or Bay Bridge, or head down the coast highway to the suburbs we would prowl that evening. Daly City, Redwood City, and San Jose were good areas; Mill Valley and the wealthier suburbs less so. Our prime area would be a subdivision that housed skilled blue-collar workers. Our prime "mooch" would be a young blue-collar worker with a wife and two small children. If we saw a swing in the front yard our eyes would gleam, and if we saw other evidence of consumer spending—such as a glimpse of an RCA color television console through the front window—we would jack up our eye-contact to laser intensity. I always preferred to have the husband answer the door—if the wife invited me in, the husband often would be suspicious, and in any event, it became more difficult to establish the necessary authority in these blue-collar families when introduced by the woman. I would wait at the front door until the husband came out of curiosity, and I would make my introduction then.

My introduction invariably was that I was taking a survey. I was not selling encyclopedias; the company would hardly waste someone of my talents as a door-to-door salesman. No, I was doing market research. Nobody sells encyclopedias anymore, and nobody has since the invention of the "Collier

Qualifier" in 1954. Instead, thousands of sets of encyclopedias of various brands have been "placed" with "qualified families" as part of an ongoing effort to test consumer reactions to whatever "revolutionary, new home research center" the representative happens to be studying.

The salesman is, of course, doing no such thing; he is selling a set of books, often an inferior encyclopedia that has not been updated in twenty years. The genius of the "Collier Qualifier" is that it simultaneously solves several basic problems of the door-to-door salesman. First it defuses the suspicion that the representative is a salesman by transforming him into a survey-taker. This is one reason why college students were in such demand as representatives. First, they carry with them emanations of sincerity and academia. Second, the qualifier throws the ball right back into the buyer's court. The representative is not selling books, heavens no, he is looking for "qualified" people to receive them *free*. By casually titillating the householder's greed, he shifts the roles of pursuer and pursued. Third, the anxiety is created that the homeowner might miss out on something "new and revolutionary" in "home research materials." The salesman would suggest that the "reference service" to be surveyed had something to do with computers, and allowed the encyclopedia to be "brought instantly up to date" at any moment. It is difficult to overstate the importance of this fraudulent claim. At different points in the pitch, this claim served different purposes. Initially, at the door, we allowed the buyer to believe that if he did not qualify for the free set of books, the Joneses next door might end up the beneficiary of this "state of the art" research center.

Although the reality of the encyclopedia was far more mundane than the illusions we were spinning, we were in fact "qualifying" families with our little surveys at the doorstep. Anyone who let us in after hearing our three-minute spiel at the door was a setup for the rest of the pitch. Conversely, it was better to be turned away at the door than to get three-quarters of the way through a forty-five-minute pitch before finding that the family was "unqualified." Although the introduction sounds corny and phony, it is amazing how effective it is. We found that the qualifier might even be used successfully on a family more than once. I sold encyclopedias to people who already had a set of books sitting in the living room. Occasionally I used to play by trying out the spiel on sophisticated and cynical friends. I found that I was seriously engaging the attention of people with whom I had just been discussing the corruption of door-to-door sales. Testimony to the effectiveness of the pitch is that in recent years it has been outlawed in several states.

Occasionally someone would suggest that we conduct the survey on the doorstep. We never gave the pitch in these circumstances. For one thing, standing on the doorstep places the salesman in an awkward, insecure position relative to the potential customer. To allow the customer to keep you there would be to cede him too much authority and conversely diminish your own. On the other hand, when the customer lets you into his living room, he is recognizing the salesman's authority—admitting the salesman into his sanctum. Rather than an intruder, the salesman becomes an honored guest. We always accepted a cup of coffee, if offered, which further sealed a bond of intimacy with the buyer and enhanced our image as honored guest.

The persuasive power of the pitch is that it speaks past the rational, sophisticated side of the potential customer and taps certain primal anxieties. The introduction silences alarms and allows the message of the pitch to get past the defenses that protect the customer from these basic anxieties. In the case of the "Collier Qualifier," these anxieties have to do with the "mooch's" education and, more broadly, with his sense of his place in society. The pitch operates by manipulating the talismanic powers the word "education" has for most Americans. During the survey, the representative asks the husband and wife how well they can keep up with the fast pace of the modern world, with all the new developments in the different sciences, and so on. Even to ponder such a question is to accept it as valid, and once accepted, it is impossible for the average person to answer it satisfactorily.

No one can keep pace with change today; the effect of the question is to educe the anxiety, never far from the surface in most people, that the world is leaving them behind. And so the salesman enters the customer's house, with the customer's mind on things other than the fact that an unexpected stranger, with a briefcase and a hard sell, is interrupting his evening, later to walk away with a signed contract entitling his company to more than $500 of the customer's money. California, in an attempt to control the abuses of the "Collier Qualifier," passed a law that gives the customer twenty-four hours to back out of the contract. But such is the power of the pitch that only a small percentage of sales go bad in this way.

Once in the house, the salesman expands upon the theme of the difficulties of keeping up with the pace of change, and also introduces the idea that children without access to a means of keeping up-to-date will find themselves hopelessly disadvantaged in the ruthless competition for jobs. The salesman uses children as a foil for amplifying the guilts and insecurities for which the pitch has been probing. When the salesman says, "only educated kids can survive in today's ruthlessly competitive world," the parents are prodded to think that only access to knowledge can save their children from a life of plodding mediocrity and dullness. If the family sits through this most insulting part of the pitch, there is a very good probability that they will become customers.

I might not have paid particular attention to the power of these anxieties associated with education were it not for the fact that during the summer I was selling encyclopedias George Wallace was also tapping this same power source for different purposes. Before heading out West I had spent some months studying the Wallace campaign of '68. What struck me then was that the same people who ritually exorcised the intellectual elite of America during a Wallace rally were a perfect constituency for my sales pitch. In fact, not a few of the people I sold encyclopedias to were Wallace sympathizers. It might seem strange that people who would roar approval of Wallace as he attacked "over-educated know-nothings who wouldn't know what to do at the scene of an accident" would then willingly fork over five hundred dollars for an encyclopedia in the hope that this might enable their offspring to join that cursed elite. But the answer was supplied in November when Wallace's astonishing popularity evaporated, as people returned to the real world to vote.

The theater of the Wallace rally was just that: theater. Wallace's anti-intellectualism did not indicate a rebellion against the rationalism of Washington and American society; rather, it reflected frustrations born of the power intellect has over our lives. The real world was buying an encyclopedia and hoping its children might advance their station in the meritocracy. The Wallace movement, like its unlikely age-mate, the Black Power movement, was the protest of drowning people. Faced with a choice of betting on Wallace who promised to overthrow the ivory tower, and on an encyclopedia which might promise entrance, the Wallacites I encountered bet on the Establishment.

That summer, however, not yet having the evidence of November 4, when Wallace's support evaporated, I had to figure out the anomaly with the evidence supplied by the Wallace rally and the sales pitch. Both sought to harness the power source inherent in anxieties about education. In the Wallace rally these anxieties were personified (as the "double-dome bureaucrats who know how to run your life better than you do"), and then purged through ridicule. In the sales pitch these anxieties were educed and amplified; then the buyer was offered release through the purchase for the painless price of a dime a day (an aspect of the sales pitch we shall get to in a moment). The constituency of the Wallace rally, gaining courage from its mass, hectored these anxieties.

During the sales pitch, the blue-collar buyer had no such mass support. In qualifying for the pitch, the family had abandoned its defenses and accredited—by admitting the salesman to their living room—the authority of the intellect and, as well, the authority of the intellectual. This inconsistency between the homage paid to the intellect through the encyclopedia purchase and the contempt manifest in the

Wallace rally suggests that whether or not it is behaviorally resolved through the purchase, the relationship between this blue-collar constituency and the intellect is poorly integrated.

THE BLUE-COLLAR WORKER
AND THE INTELLECTUAL ESTABLISHMENT

And no wonder. Here was one case where Vice-President Agnew's analysis was correct. In 1968 it was culturally insupportable for a workman to work with his hands and feel good about it. The climate has changed somewhat since then, but even now, the primary anxiety of a democracy is that for the white man, whose station is presumed to be limited only by his brains and industry, those locked into an hourly wage must suffer the anxiety that they are working with their hands because they do not have the intelligence to be one of the movers and shakers of society. This anxiety only increases as mass-production techniques and compartmentalization remove all opportunities for imagination or artistry from work. The insincere recognition and scant respect our society confers upon all but the most skilled workers leaves the average person with insubstantial piers upon which to build an identity. More important, from the point of view of the salesman, these insubstantial piers leave the worker prey for the "Collier Qualifier."

Although the worker can establish his excellence through his extracurricular activities (best batting average in the softball league; largest collection of deer antlers in Berkshire County), the most popular way for the American to redeem his life is through his children. Children are the materialistic equivalent of the Hindu notion of reincarnation. Rather than advancing in the next life through virtue, we use the upward mobility of our children to validate lives deemed inconsequential by the meritocracy. Thus the anxieties probed by the sales pitch have a double reference. The salesman summons doubts about the buyer's performance in this achievement-oriented society, and then stimulates an unconscious association in the buyer, reassuring the husband and wife that the blinding light of their children's success will obscure their own failures in this rationalistic world.

It was absurd to believe that the encyclopedia I was selling might be the *deus ex machina* that would lift children out of the benighted reaches of the lower middle class, or that its purchase alone might keep the family up-to-date. Yet that is precisely what the pitch suggested, and precisely how the encyclopedia was perceived. The literature I brought with me showed how the books looked in their "handsome" maple book rack. The literature showed some of the four-color illustrations and photographs that enhanced the articles. A few weeks after I began selling, I finally got a look at a set of the New Standard Encyclopedia. It looked like a set of bound magazines. I quit the next day and went to work for the Encyclopaedia Britannica (who used the same pitch). The New Standard was probably the worst encyclopedia being marketed that year. Certainly, it is reasonable to expect that should a salesman stimulate families into thinking about an encyclopedia, they would then shop around before spending $500. But this was not the case. In the thrall of the sales pitch, people did not behave rationally.

THE SALES DECISION:
WHAT THE CONSUMER BUYS

In most of the homes where I "placed" encyclopedias, there was little evidence of any other reading material. It is true that this circumstance indicated that such buyers might be less prepared to judge the relative merits of encyclopedias, but I also felt that the absence of other reading material left such customers exceedingly vulnerable to the anxiety-provoking aspects of the pitch. That I often sold to this group validated this suspicion, because it would appear that a family without books had come to the conclusion that they had no need for them. I spoke about the pace of change, and the danger of being left forever behind; these families had no place to look other than to me for the abatement of these anxieties. Again it should be clear how unreasonable this whole process was. If indeed this family was gradually losing touch with new developments, a subscription to a news magazine would better keep them up-to-date than my set of books. But by now my encyclopedia had become magical, and I had the family hostage to the anxieties I had summoned.

As I probed the family for insecurities, the sales pitch would simultaneously excite their greed. The encyclopedia was not for sale, only a "qualified" family could have one, and those "qualified families" got the books for free. The only obligation was that they must display their commitment to knowledge by agreeing to keep the encyclopedia up-to-date. They did this by subscribing to the "reference service" for a dime a day. "How long would you like to keep the encyclopedia up-to-date, Mrs. Jones?" (Most women at this point would compute the remaining time until their children finished their education.) "Fifteen years? Oh, I'm sorry but the company can only take a beating like this for at most ten years, but is that all right? Fine!" This dime-a-day reference charge ended up costing the "mooch" between $450 and $550. Moreover, we would gently point out that paying a dime a day placed a large burden on both the family and the company for bookkeeping, and that it would be much easier if the family discharged their obligation in a year or eighteen months. The pitch would finish with the family signing a contract which stated the total amount they would be paying, as well as the amount of the monthly installments, and yet, even then, most families thought they were getting the books free.

After I established my credentials as a salesman, I was allowed to peek behind the veil of *maya* woven by the pitch to see what the reference service actually consisted of. One man in Chicago would send one of a dozen all-purpose answers in response to questions sent in. However, there were so few inquiries that he usually had nothing to do.

Again, to be reasonable, it would seem that after spending $500 for the "reference service" of an encyclopedia advertised as a means of preventing one's children from being left behind by the pace of change, the consumer would try to get his money's worth. But he rarely did, and I suspect that the tendency of buyers to ignore the encyclopedia and its reference service after the sale is related to the circumstances of the sale.

Appealing to the family's greed (free books) offers them a convenient fiction by which they can tuck away the doubts and insecurities the salesman has tapped, doubts which during the pitch drench both the encyclopedia and its shabby sales campaign with numinous power. The nature of the product is subordinate to the archetypal anxieties with which it is associated during the pitch, and thus, following this logic through, we might expect that the customer's good deal also has something to do with those archetypal properties, rather than with the dollar value of the product. What the customer buys with his purchase is a ticket back to the dormancy from which he has been aroused. The purchaser is activated by the pitch into performing his role in a consumer society; a sales-resistant family on a shoestring budget is transformed by the pitch into an avid consumer of the unnecessary.

Since the buyer is purchasing release from anxiety rather than a set of books, this ritual is consummated with the purchase of the books, rather than with their later use. The purchase temporarily abates those anxieties, and with the abatement of the anxieties one principal motivation for the use of the books is also diminished. Thus, the encyclopedia purchased because it offered redemption for the parents and salvation for the children sits there in its cheap case gathering dust. An informal survey I took suggests that people who were not book-oriented before the purchase of an encyclopedia, do not become so as a result of its purchase, whether the encyclopedia is the New Standard or the Encyclopaedia Britannica. Furthermore, the circumstances of the sale not only do not abate the anxieties that authored the encyclopedia's purchase but actually militate against the encyclopedia's use once purchased.

The sales pitch is clearly a rip-off, yet it was not my experience to encounter families who went through with the

sale and then later admitted they had been gypped (especially
so with the better sets of encyclopedias). For one thing, to
admit that they were gypped requires a confrontation with
those anxieties that the purchase allowed the family to avoid.
Given the cost of the encyclopedias when weighed against the
discretionary income of the average buyer, not to sense
immediately that one has been gypped requires a considerable
degree of self-deception. The purchase is the payment of
protection money for the buyer's self-esteem, and, as in any
protection racket, the victim is unlikely to point an accusing
finger for fear of the threat.

The sales pitch taps deep anxieties, but the purchase does
no more than temporarily retire them. As noted, the circumstances of the sale consecrate the books in such a way that
their very purchase becomes a wall against their future use.
Following such a purchase the buyer subsides into the uneasy
peace from which he was aroused by the sales pitch. Which
means that soon after such a pitch the consumer is ripe to be
tapped again, if not for an encyclopedia, then for another
product whose sales campaign similarly exploits the unconscious. One girl's apartment served as poignant testimony to
this phenomenon. Almost bare of furnishings, it housed three
different sets of encyclopedias. Seeing this, I didn't have the
heart to "place" with her a set of the Great Books.

THE ROLE OF THE CONSUMER DECISION
IN A CONSUMER SOCIETY

If nothing else, the above description of an encyclopedia sales
pitch explains my earlier teasing suggestion that the reason
we continue to fall prey to salesmen and sales pitches we
objectively see as corrupt is that we are not ourselves during a
pitch. We are really under a spell. How else can we explain the
absurd beliefs and irrational behavior that characterize the
consumer during the pitch? The buyer simultaneously sus-
pends his Yankee common sense and even (when faced with
the contract) disbelieves the evidence of his own eyes in his

panic to purchase an item which, before the arrival of the salesman, he had not entertained the idea of purchasing. (Often upon entering I was told, "Don't bother trying to sell us an encyclopedia, because we aren't interested.") The salesman is talking to a part of the consumer that the consumer has no access to, and hence cannot control. I believe it is the enormous frustration surrounding our manipulation by people we know to be corrupt that accounts for our schizophrenic behavior toward salesmen. We cannot dislodge them from our lives because they are trading in a currency we are only dimly aware of. In fact salesmen themselves have only the most superficial understanding of the sales pitch. It is not necessary for the salesman to understand the pitch for it to work, and so I should qualify my use of the word manipulation. Salesmen indeed manipulate their buyers, but they are mere agents. The identity of the true manipulator will be revealed later.

Let us take for a moment another perspective on the phenomenon evident in the sales pitch. That we are in a spell during a sales pitch challenges the center of our image of rational man. Moreover, in this spell we can discover both the links between modern and primitive societies as well as the critical differences between ourselves and our primitive forebears. The transaction I have described here is supremely impractical. Moreover, it is difficult to describe the purchase of the New Standard Encyclopedia through the "Collier Qualifier" as the result of autonomous judgment. Rather the whole point of the pitch is to suspend the buyer's rational, autonomous judgment, and while the alarms are silenced, to get these books in through the back door. Keep in mind that this is a decision that in the case of the encyclopedia alone represents a significant proportion of the buyer's discretionary income. In one of this buyer's more significant impingements upon the economic life of the consumer society, the buyer is not acting autonomously.

The production of the books and the money that goes into their purchase represent an expenditure of energy and resources. The purchase money is energy in trust—ultimately it will perform some work. Yet, the net result of the interchange is really that both parties retain a psychic stability. (As noted earlier, the salesman, too, preserves his identity through the sale.) The difference between the excessively large amount of energy represented in the sale and the actual worth of the books ($550 gets you books that cost $25 to produce), represents energy and resources consumed merely to maintain a psychic status quo.

Most primitive societies conserve this stability through religion: fears, doubts, and hopes, demonified and deified, are accommodated with a minimum disruption of the biosphere. Yet here, in the "Collier Qualifier," an anxiety that is fundamentally religious—doubt over one's place in the scheme of things—is translated into a material appetite. We may not be rational but, as we shall see, we are primitive in a different way from the aborigine.

To develop this same point, we might look at this purchase from yet another perspective. An observer ignorant of the internal dynamic of the sale would see a buyer use his accumulated money to purchase an article that then sits unused in the living room. The observer might leap to the conclusion that the object, since it served no obvious purpose, was a religious object, an idol of some sort, and that the transaction involved some form of devotion. The observer might then assume that the entire encyclopedia industry, with its presses, lumber and paper suppliers, research and sales network, existed to service the buyer's appetite for encyclopedias, and also, that the buyer's livelihood—his daily efforts to accumulate some surplus—is largely devoted to enabling him to pay for this appetite. And so the face of the world is transformed—by the encyclopedia company and its related industries on the one hand, and by the work that helps the buyer to accumulate surplus on the other—in the servicing of this religious need.

Now, our purposefully ignorant observer, pursuing the nature of this strange religion, might at this point try to characterize the spectrum of activities that are tributary to this devotion and other devotions like it in an attempt to fathom the nature of this religion. This is where things get interesting.

Because, although I did not know this at the time I was puzzling over the structure of the encyclopedia purchase, there is a pattern that relates the structure of the various transactions that characterize daily life in a consumer society, and also a pattern to the transformations wrought in the world as a result of these transactions. When I describe the purchase as occurring when the buyer's rational judgment is suspended, or use the word irrational to describe the consumer decision, I do not mean to imply that such decisions are either chaotic or random. On the contrary, during the sales pitch the consumer is "tricked" by a consumer culture into performing a role vital to the health of that culture. The consumer's money and his oft-repeated purchase decisions are the fuel of a consumer society; transformations accomplished as a result of the consumer's purchase give the society its shape. The company and the naive Marxist critic both might say that the purpose of the transaction is to swell profits. Although this may be the primary concern of the New Standard Encyclopedia Company, it is not the purpose of the transaction. As we shall see, both the seller and the buyer are answerable to the needs of the aggregate consumer culture. The transformations are the "work" of the purchase, and the purpose of this "work" will become clear as we probe deeper into the nature of consumer behavior.

However, to understand the cultural architecture that organizes consumer purchases requires that we go both sideways and backward—first to consider some of the broad contrasts that differentiate the consumer from the nonconsumer and then to delve into the past in search of the antecedents of consumer behavior and the pressures that eventually produced it. The next chapter considers an anomaly that suggests that consumer behavior is more deeply embedded in our character than we might think or like to admit. This anomaly is the case of Yankees in paradise, people who, to their horror, discover that a consumer society is not something you can simply leave.

~ 2 ~

Tahiti: Illusory Refuge from the Consumer Society

"You live in a thatch hut with the daughter of the king, a slim young maiden in whose eyes is an ancient wisdom. Her breasts are golden speckled pears, her belly a melon, and her odor is like nothing so much as a jungle fern. In the evening, on the blue lagoon, under the silvery moon, to your love you croon in the soft sylabelew and vocabelew of her langorour tongorour. Your body is golden brown like hers, and tourists have need of the indignant finger of the missionary to point you out. They envy you your breech clout and carefree laugh and little brown bride and fingers instead of forks. But you don't return their envy, and when a beautiful society girl comes to your hut in the night, seeking to learn the secret of your happiness, you send her back to her yacht that hangs on the horizon like a nervous race horse. And so you dream away the days, fishing, hunting, dancing, swimming, kissing, and picking flowers to twine in your hair . . .

"'Well, my friend, what do you think of the South Seas?'"

Miss Lonelyhearts
—*Nathanael West*

Other societies create refugees through conquest or political or religious oppression. We create refugees through a poorly defined set of pressures that have to do with our very affluence and freedom. For generations the affluent society has spun off refugees, people unwilling or unable any longer to cope with the oppression of modern life. Their number is increasing, and for every man or woman who flees the country altogether, there are several who achieve some compromise solution by quitting the city for the country, or hedging their commitment to their jobs, or by getting back to the earth, or otherwise simplifying their life-style. A Stanford Research Center study places the number of people who have "voluntarily" simplified their lives by leaving the city or voluntarily taking a lower level job at between 10–20 million.

Today, and for generations before the current exodus, one cynosure for the refugee from the rigors of modern life has been Polynesia. Although the number of Americans who have attempted to live there is small, the image of the expatriate life in Tahiti has had enduring allure for the refugee from the consumer society and the paradisal sonority of the word Polynesia is influential far beyond what might be justified by the actual number of expatriates who have attempted to settle there. Polynesia is a powerful symbol of escape.

The number of expatriates might be far greater, if the French who administer Polynesia did not do everything short of sealing the borders to discourage immigrants. As it is there are now only 249 American residents in French Polynesia— less than a hundred families in all—and those who live there tend to be affluent, because it is very difficult for an American to obtain a job that might be filled by a Tahitian or a Frenchman. For all these qualifications, the small American expatriate group in Tahiti holds a numinous place in the American unconscious. They have attempted to do what most of us at some time or other considered doing. How have they fared?

The answer is, not too well. While Tahitians manage to pass their days on these small islands without dissatisfaction, few of the Americans who come to live here adapt successfully. Rather, many deteriorate; they turn to drink, their lives fall into disorder; and eventually, if they do not completely destroy themselves, they return home. People, who for the most part come to Tahiti to flee the complexities of modern life, seem to have difficulty adjusting to the one place where their dream of a simple, untrammeled, and secure existence is within grasp. Move beyond the touristy environs of Papeete and it is still easy to secure a comfortable subsistence with minimal effort. Arguments might be advanced that if the Americans there do deteriorate, it is because Polynesia has changed and disappoints the dreamer, or because Polynesia attracts expatriates already on the downswing before they arrive, or because the French there make it difficult for the American to do anything meaningful, or for any number of reasons pertaining to the changed circumstances of the islands or the peculiarities of the Americans who migrate there. While circumstance, to a degree, does complicate the life of the expatriate, it does not account fully for this curious inability to find happiness in paradise. Rather than look to circumstance to account for this, we are eventually forced to look at the needs the expatriates bring with them from the United States to the islands.

Upon examination, it turns out that these needs are bound up with the very pressures that drove many of the expatriates to Polynesia in the first place, and this is what makes the consideration of expatriate malaise worthwhile in a study of the nature of consumer behavior. By eliminating various possible explanations of expatriate problems it becomes clear that, far from being circumstantial, the malaise of the expatriate in Polynesia has to do with the very structure upon which the wealth and power of his home society is built. That structure is what I call the consumer personality, a set of needs and relationships to the material world which is shared even by those who flee. And it is only when the consumer is placed in an environment in which his way of life is alien that some of the properties of the consumer personality become evident. What happens, then, to Americans in Tahiti, and why does this same malaise not afflict the Tahitians for whom Polynesia is home?

~

POLYNESIA

Tahiti itself is not as simple as its image as a refuge suggests. French Polynesia is a glimmering collection of atolls and islands scattered, sometimes idly, sometimes dramatically, over thousands of square miles of the Pacific. The total land area of all these islands and atolls is about the same as Rhode Island. Polynesians themselves share a common linguistic, cultural, and racial heritage, although there are marked divergences in the behavior of the peoples included in that group. The Maoris of New Zealand, the tradition-bound Samoans, the Tongans, the industrious Rarotongans, the vanishing Hawaiians, the guttural-tongued inhabitants of the Austral islands, and the Easter Islanders are all Polynesians.

The social fabric of the islands suffered the inevitable blows of "progress." The missionaries attacked with vigor the pagan practices they saw around them. More recently, the French with their ambitions of a *force de frappe* sought as a kind of bribe to develop the region which has served as a staging area for their nuclear testing, and more recently still, what remains of Tahitian culture has come under pressure from the arrival of throngs of tourists. Now a thirty-mile strip on the western shore of Tahiti is marred by pollution, hotels, tract homes, and the traffic jams that accompany tourist blight.

Nonetheless, the lure for Americans has been and still is a fleeting and nebulous quality called "The Tahitian Way of Life." There are many islands in the world, some more remote or more physically beautiful than the island and atolls of Polynesia. What is remote, alien, but achingly alluring about Polynesia is our impression of the Tahitians, not their island. The Tahitian is our daemon, our opposite, which often we would very much like to be.

I have made two trips to Tahiti, the first in 1971 while en route to an investigation of fragging in Vietnam; the second in 1976 when I wanted to explore in more detail some of the intriguing questions that coalesced around my first visit. I should say that I, like many a young man brought up in the cold and pollution of the American Northeast, used to nurture dreams as a schoolboy of fleeing to the South Seas. I read Maugham, I read Michener, and I would tell people that someday I intended to make my break for Tahiti. Michener's story "Povanaa's Daughter" made a deep impression on me then. I recently reread it. It is a nice story, though not really an accurate picture of Tahitians or their relationships with Americans. In rereading the story I was amazed at how my imagination as a youngster had transformed this tale, which in part deals with the drastically altered and reduced culture of the Tahitians, into a paradigm of a pristine and untrammeled way of life. This shock helps me to understand why expatriates come to Tahiti and decide to settle down, whereas elsewhere they would look at the tin-roofed shacks and hotels and move on, clucking over the despoliation of another civilization.

On my way to Vietnam I decided to stop off in Tahiti for a glimpse of my now-fading dream and to check on the progress of a friend who had made such a break.

Jeff Stookey was a typical American expatriate only in the sense that he came to perceive a fatal chemistry between Polynesian and expatriate lives. He graduated from Yale at the height of the Vietnam War in 1967, after an academic career that saw him rise from the bottom 10 percent to the top 2 percent of his class. Far from being decadent and aimless, Stookey was the very image of that fast-dying breed, the Ivy League gentleman. He was decent, intelligent, and courtly, and he was graduated from Yale with quite well-defined ideas of what he wanted to do in the immediate future, the first of which was to secure a 4–F by virtue of knees ruined in athletics. The second was immediately to set out upon a trip which, in three years, he hoped would take him around the world. His first stop was the Pacific, and for two years he never traveled any farther.

Stookey is still remembered with considerable affection by the longtime expatriates in Polynesia. This trustworthy, energetic, well-mannered fellow struck a responsive chord among the expatriates. He quickly learned French, and within six weeks of his arrival began to be accepted by the Tahitians. It was his fleeting associations with Polynesians that kept Stookey in Tahiti long after he planned to leave. He supported himself through odd jobs and through writing for the third- and fourth-rate publications that feed off the tourist trade in the Pacific. He left once, only to be called back from Fiji by Jim Boyack, who wanted Stookey to help him begin publishing an English-language newspaper. Then he left for good, and he has never been back. Why?

He left partly because he had unfulfilled ambitions and partly because he noticed that most of the expatriates he was associated with were slowly falling to pieces. The mind-dissolving torpidity of Polynesia worried Stookey. "Ten years seemed to be the critical amount of time," said Stookey. "After ten years they would quite quickly begin to go downhill." I asked him why he thought this happened. "Because," he said simply, "it is very difficult for an American to adjust to a place where nothing matters."

Many of those who went to Tahiti were looking for a place where they might be forgotten by the world, and I would be foolish to deny that this wish did not constitute a portion of my own dreams of Polynesia. But I knew before I went to Tahiti that this refuge was not for me, not yet anyway. Still, I was intrigued by the question of my deteriorating compatriots. And so in 1971 I stopped in this lotus-land during my odyssey to Vietnam to probe my adolescent dreams as lived by others. And even though I had armed myself with intellectual detachment, I still considered abandoning my assignment and staying in Polynesia. But I went on, and then five years later I came back to explore further this mysterious cultural pocket in the Pacific and its deadly relationship with American lives.

OUR DAEMONS: A PLACE WHERE NOTHING MATTERS

That Tahitians have been stripped of so many of the external accoutrements of their culture over the past two hundred years somewhat simplifies the task of identifying those remaining characteristics to which Americans respond. That is: through relationships with Tahitians, the expatriate senses the opportunity to partake of a charmed world. Perhaps the most obvious characteristic is the physical appearance of the Tahitians. Tahitians are among the largest people on earth. By middle age both men and women tend to be immensely broad, although during their adolescence and early adulthood, they are strikingly graceful. Moreover, accounts of Tahitian sexuality suggest nothing as overheated as the activities prevalent at the local Club Med on Morea. Rather, the expatriates are seduced by the Tahitians' promise of life before the Fall, of a childlike existence where people are unimpressed by success and are nonjudgmental of failure. It is a place, as Stookey said, where nothing matters. Strivers are looked upon as deranged. It is childhood again, with nature as the warm, protective mother, and the adult twist of vibrant, accommodating women. It is, in short, the exact opposite of the consumer societies at home. And so they come.

THE EXPATRIATES

"My life was getting a little too complicated in the States. I like the fact that it's simple here, but I do find it a little suffocating with regard to ambition." This from a successful entrepreneur.

"One reason I came here was to get away from the American economy . . . I don't want to live anywhere where you have to lock your door . . . I came here to work two days a week, but demand for sails is keeping me too busy . . . my whole movement is toward a simpler, more self-reliant life-style . . . eventually I want to farm on an outer island . . ." This from a quiet, slightly paunchy sailmaker, who has been here four years. A copy of *Small Is Beautiful* is on his table.

"I came here looking for dreams of the South Pacific. . . . I intended to move on to another spot, but we got demasted . . . yes, this place is changing, but it is changing slower than anywhere else. . . ." This from a marine biologist who has been here six years.

"I worked in Universal City as an art director. . . . I began to wonder what my values were and realized that LA was not one of them. Essentially I live in Samoa and we've just been passing through for the past year. . . ." This from a middle-aged, hip Californian who lives on his trimaran.

"I came in '56 intending to leave, but I didn't leave until 1959. I did research, then I retired in 1960. Since then we have stayed half the time here, half in Tahoe."

"I intended to stay two weeks, I stayed two years. . . ."

"I intended to stay a few months, I've been here twenty-five years."

"Like everyone else I did not intend to stay, but now it's over twenty years."

"I intended just to stay six months, but we've been here thirty-one years."

But simply coming to Tahiti does not guarantee entrance into this charmed world.

American expatriates, although a small group themselves, fall into subgroups. There are the wealthy who make regular trips back to the United States and who could leave at any time and pick up where they left off at home. There is a small but growing group of people of retirement age, for whom Tahiti is a pleasant place to spend their later years. Again, many members of this group return to the United States regularly, and most of them do not regard their decision to move here as any sort of break with the consumer society at home. From the French point of view, these first two groups are the ideal Americans to have around.

Less desirable from the French view, but more interesting, are the younger, poorer expatriates, who abandon careers or families or futures and manage to slip through the scrutiny of French immigration and establish a foothold in Polynesia. There are not many who fit this description, perhaps seventy-five Americans, and an equal number of other nationalities. Rounding out the profile of American expatriates are those in Polynesia on a temporary assignment, either working in the tourist trade or working for American-run ventures.

Some of these people choose to stay on in Tahiti, but the

hard-core expatriates are the few score who have linked their destiny to Tahiti, a group for the most part unwanted by the French, though many are popular among the Tahitians. This group includes only a very few women, and not many in the group could be said to have successfully adapted to the islands.

Gordon Knight is about forty, and he does not quite fit the image of the poor American expatriate. His wife, from whom he is now separated, is Tahitian and quite well off in her own right. He met his wife in Hawaii, moved to Tahiti, and here he has been for the past eight years. After a few years working for a bank, Knight switched to selling Hobie Cats, the catamaran equivalent of the Sunfish. He does quite well. He has built an elaborate version of the traditional thatch Tahitian compound in the ritzy Punaiuai district south of Papeete. Knight is better educated, better-off, and more reflective than most expatriates. He is self-examining and he appears capable of assessing his situation and the changes that have occurred in Tahiti with some detachment. He is also approaching the critical ten-year mark and he is getting uneasy.

He likes the simplicity of life here. He feels that as a result of living in Tahiti he gets "uptight less now" and "lives moments" as they come along. "I am not so much money-motivated now." . . . In Tahiti, says Knight, the astonishing discovery is that "you don't have to search for things, because they are here."

Which, one would think, is all a person ever needs. But then, creeping at the edge of Knight's thoughts are doubts. "Every once in a while you feel, I'm forty; what have I done? I'm happy, but I haven't done a thing." Because of this Knight is thinking of leaving Tahiti. In Knight's case there is something else to crystallize his thoughts on Tahiti: his children. There is probably no better place on earth to bring up young children. However, "The place does not prepare you to survive . . . a child has to be exposed to more. . . ." Now that his children are getting older, Knight is beginning to find Tahiti "a little *enfermé*."

Jim Boyack founded, with Jeff Stookey's help, the *Tahiti*

Bulletin, an English-language daily newspaper that serves the tourists and tourist industry. Boyack, a tall angular man, is a former poet—a product of the Beat era—and an expatriate who left the United States with the firm intention of leaving the consumer society behind. He discovered Tahiti by accident when he was twenty-two, "the Tahiti," he recently wrote, "I believed in so much I gave it my youth." It was Boyack who showed me around Tahiti during my first visit in 1971. At that time, he, his wife, and their two little girls lived a few miles north of Papeete. Back then, I spent my first four days living in the rundown Hotel Stuart, a dump which has been the first home in Tahiti for a number of the islands' famous expatriate émigrés. Boyack suggested I move into the offices of the *Tahiti Bulletin.* Making my home on a couch in the offices of a newspaper was actually a step up from the Hotel Stuart. During the day, Boyack would drive me around while volubly addressing the question of expatriate life in Tahiti. He approached expatriate life in Tahiti from every conceivable angle and quite often contradicted himself as he did so. He was obviously in love with Polynesia, but he was also a student of the dangers and signs of expatriate disintegration. Quite a few of the people I met would have been surprised to learn that Boyack had introduced us with the idea that he was showing me a case study in expatriate deterioration.

Boyack, who had presumably fled the consumer society, and who professed to want no part of the rat-race in America, turned out to be one of the most adept entrepreneurs to hit Tahiti. He came to Tahiti to help run the magazine, *O Tahiti,* owned by another American expatriate, Buzz Miller. Against Miller's advice and wishes Boyack started the *Bulletin.* The newspaper became far more successful than Miller's magazine.

I did not see Boyack on my second trip to Tahiti, although, while I was there, he still owned the *Tahiti Bulletin.* Boyack had left Tahiti for New Zealand. This surprised me, because while Boyack was acutely aware of the dangers facing the expatriate and the changes that afflict the islands, he had been absolutely committed to staying. Just before I left for Vietnam in 1971, Boyack reviewed the pros and cons of the expatriate life and then said, "But the important thing is that I wake up in the morning and I go to work without poisoning myself in an atmosphere of hate and violence. I live in a place where my kids can grow up healthy and free, and I come home to privacy and peace. Really, what more could I want?"

At that time I thought the question, "What more could I want?" was purely rhetorical. Evidently it was not. "Boyack has had it with Tahiti," said one of his friends. "He just comes in now to transact his business in the shortest possible time and then returns to New Zealand. Tahiti has become too small for Jim; there are too few things to do, to see, and to buy." Several expatriates remarked separately to me that "The Americans who come to Tahiti are people who can't make it anywhere else in the world." It is true that Tahiti has long had the reputation as a refuge for those who want to forget their failures. And there is also a tradition in the fiction of Tahiti of portraying Polynesia as a place where the broken-down refuse of the West is restored and sent back to do battle. There are cases of this happening, but perhaps more interesting are the cases of those such as Boyack who "make it" in Tahiti, having come there to flee the rigors of the consumer's life.

There is some irony in the fact that many of the expatriates support themselves by abetting the tourist industry and other aspects of the development of the islands, bringing the very changes they came to escape. During my first visit one expatriate remarked, "The Americans who cry the loudest about pollution and the changing face of the islands are the ones making a buck off it. They came here to get away from America and they are bringing all the problems of America with them."

The tourist industry provides one of the few outlets in Polynesia for what might be termed the expatriate's American-ness. To industriously try to exploit this outlet often alienates the expatriate from his refuge, and, moreover, can leave him with the nightmare feeling that he is spreading the seed of that which he came to Tahiti to escape. On the other hand, to eschew entrepreneurial opportunities is to court the uneasy feelings shared by Gordon Knight and many others that the world is passing them by while they waste their talents in Tahiti.

With one exception, I did not meet the expatriate for whom the physical beauty of Tahiti and its people and the satisfactions of somatic needs were sufficient reward, as they are for Tahitians.

Far more numerous than expatriates for whom the islands become too small as a result of success achieved in Tahiti are those expatriates who were established in the States before they came to Tahiti. Among the expatriates during Stookey's time there was a rule of thumb: that one might stay two years soaking up what Tahiti offered and still leave, but if the expatriate stayed ten years he would never leave, because by then he was unfit to live anywhere else. There was also a rule of thumb concerning writers. To wit: that the writer who stayed six months in Tahiti might finish a novel; two years, and he might write a chapter; ten years, and he wouldn't write a line. Both these dictums fall into the general category of decline referred to as Pacific Paralysis.

Pete Palmer is the current model for such deterioration in Tahiti. He came to Tahiti from the West Coast in the mid-1960s, deciding at that point to throw over a successful career in business for the good life of Tahiti. He also felt that the United States had become unlivable, a conclusion he reached from a conservative, not radical, perspective. Palmer's chosen method of destruction is drink, a means popular with expatriates. He is a member of a roving circle of expatriates who circulate slowly through the bars of Papeete, feeding off each other's weakness.

Palmer is married to a Tahitian and has three kids. He is thoroughly disgusted with the Americanization of the islands and with the Americanization of his own life. For five years he has been threatening to move to another Polynesian island, but he has yet to act on his threats. It was Palmer who back in 1967 told Stookey some of the folk wisdom of Pacific Paralysis, and it has become clear that Palmer is in the terminal stages of the malady. These might be summarized as follows:

1. *There is no intellectual stimulation*
2. *The world is passing me by*
3. *The Tahiti that greeted me when I first came no longer exists*
4. *Loose ends back home*
5. *Nobody cares about what I've accomplished*

To map isomorphically the personality that could be inferred from characteristic "complaints" of expatriates would leave the misleading impression that the expatriate's problem is infantilism or egoism. If, however, these complaints are examined as the result of tensions deriving from an inappropriate mapping of a personality bred in one set of circumstances onto a cultural environment responsive to different circumstances, it becomes clear that expatriate malaise is not mere character deficiency. Earlier I noted that expatriates who would be described as successes in terms of the consumer society at home seem to have problems adapting to Tahiti similar to the problems of those who are clearly failures. To restate this a little differently: while "character deficiency" (as measured against the well-adapted consumer at home) might have something to do with getting the expatriate to Tahiti, it does not explain why expatriates deteriorate once there. This brings us back to the alternate explanation.

By experience, zoos have discovered that putting a leopard in even a quite large cage will still produce neurotic behavior if the animal does not have enough vertical space in which to exercise by climbing and jumping. Floor area, though it might seem ample, leaves the leopard no place to express his leopardness. The same might be said for the expatriates in Tahiti. It may seem like a perfect refuge, but it lacks something expatriates need. Though they may feel that they are abandoning the consumer society by expatriating to Polynesia, that society is a more profound part of the expatriate's personality than most would care to admit. The expatriate brings with him certain unconscious expectations and needs that are unanswered by either the physical or cultural climate of Tahiti. The satisfaction of those expectations and needs is essential to the expatriate's identity—his sense of his place in the world. In the neglectful world of Polynesia, these piers begin to crumble. Or, if the expatriate chooses to try and maintain that identity through his entrepreneurial talents, he finds himself alienated from the culture he came to Tahiti to partake of.

Some of the characteristics of the common needs and expectations of expatriates are evident if their complaints are judged as tensions with the physical and cultural environment in Polynesia. For example, expatriate frustrations with regard to intellectual stimulation have to do with placing minds that have been encouraged to be roving, questioning, and self-examining in a cultural environment that views intellectual curiosity as a pernicious threat to stability. It is another aspect of the difference between the steady-state and change-oriented society. The expatriate entrepreneurs, as well as some of the more sophisticated expatriates, create pursuits, hobbies, or games to maintain their intellectual tautness in the face of this apathy. One expatriate collects shells and art, another is compiling a concordance of Tahitian and Marquesan words, another uses the irritating routine of radio broadcasts as a type of scourging ritual to remind himself of his need for discipline. The Tahitians get by without any of these devices, and devices are what they are. The expatriates are feeding an appetite that does not exist in their Tahitian counterparts. This is not to suggest that Tahitians are stupid. Rather it seems as though the kind of intellectual curiosity that is the source of expatriate restlessness is something that is culturally activated in America and Europe and negatively reinforced in Tahiti. It is easy to see how the Tahitian culture, whose job is to define harmonious relationships between a group of people and the strictly circumscribed universe of a small island in the Pacific, might find intellectual curiosity a burden. Especially so if, as is the case, these islands gratuitously and bountifully provide for the somatic needs of the populace. The proof of this wisdom is evident in the maladaptiveness of expatriates burdened with this virus.

With regard to intellectual climate, Tahiti is the equivalent of agar, a neutral medium. Without reinforcement from the

Tahitians, the intellectual demands of expatriates are set in startling relief. In their service the expatriate seals himself off from the clement, charmed world of Polynesia as he catalogues its words or its fauna or its flora, or as he experiments with new seed variants, or as he plots entrepreneurial schemes. The pressing need to assuage this expatriate appetite organizes the expatriate's life, and this need is also manifest in the way the expatriate reorganizes his world. What we see at work in the strategies the expatriates employ to maintain mental tautness is the alienating power of the Western intellect. In the Tahitian setting, where intellectual curiosity is only marginally necessary to survival and maladaptive to a long-term accommodation to this universe, the demands of the expatriate intellect illustrate one characteristic of the consumer personality. That is the ascendency of the intellect over the unconscious with regard to authority over behavior. In an environment like that of the consumer society at home, this ascendency is somewhat taken for granted, if for no other reason than that this relationship is an integrated part of the consumer culture and is responsive to its demands. That the intellect continues to maintain its hegemony in a place without such cultural or environmental reinforcements, a place with little for the intellect to feed on and little need for the interventions of technology, suggests that this relationship is a more profound part of the personality than we might at first suspect.

Most expatriates arrive in Tahiti with the expectation (to echo the travel brochures) that Tahiti is not merely a place but a state of mind. It must be disheartening for the expatriate to discover that this applies to the consumer society at home as well. The expatriate is equipped to survive amid change. He is equipped to encourage change, or at least that is one conclusion evident in expatriate behavior in Polynesia.

The change orientation of the expatriate is a basic tension between the expatriate and the Tahitian, and it is easy to see how it opens out into some other manifestations of expatriate malaise. The change-oriented aspect of consumer societies is in part expressed through the notion of upward mobility. This in turn emphasizes material and quantitative measures of status as a means of determining how far one has progressed and who one is. Here again we can see the intellect mediating the consumer expatriate's experience of his own identity. The consumer experiences selfhood through a rational grid which reflects the aspirations of the aggregate consumer society. In Polynesia, where identity is not experienced so objectively, no one really cares about the different kinds of status to which the expatriate may feel he is entitled. Similarly, the Tahitian does not feel that the world is passing him by, for he does not view life as a struggle for advancement in which others will get ahead if he does not keep up the pace.

In summary, the argument so far is that something other than ordinary expatriate problems like "strange customs" interferes with the expatriate's experience of Tahiti which does not interfere in the case of the Tahitians. Something disappoints the expatriate, prevents him from enjoying the paradise which seems within his grasp. That something is a property of the expatriate personality, and not merely a circumstantial coincidence applying to a number of expatriates. That something has been characterized as a type of restless intellectual curiosity responsive to and in need of a cultural and physical environment somewhat different from that of Polynesia. Further, this intellectual curiosity is not, as is commonly assumed, the rare and happy accident of a Western education, but rather a broad phenomenon, indicative of a relationship between the individual and the world around him shared by American expatriates regardless of their educational background. One aspect of this relationship considered has been the "change-orientation" of the expatriates and the transformative role played by the expatriate intellect. This contrasts with the relatively passive role of the Tahitian intellect in its environment.

However, there is a grand irony here, an irony that only becomes evident when this consumer personality is examined more closely, and when the purpose of the changes wrought by the consumer personality is uncovered. For despite the seeming diversity of the "intellectual" pursuits of the expatriates in Tahiti, the various transformations wrought by the consumer intellect have a common purpose. The irony is that the ultimate goal of this "change-oriented" personality is the creation of a refuge from change and the vicissitudes of nature.

The path through this irony, from change-orientation to dread of change is tortuous and is not readily perceivable from the evidence available in Tahiti. What is apparent from expatriate experience in Tahiti is that Americans bring something with them to the islands. The experience of expatriates in Tahiti suggests that there is something compelling about the Western perspective on the world, that it is not something idly discarded. But the communalities of expatriate disaffection suggest only the general outlines of the shared aspects of their needs. One cannot infer the design of an ant colony from the behavior of a few isolated ants. The simple question of why expatriates can't find happiness in Tahiti demands a consideration of the structure of the expatriate's personality, and from there, a consideration of the structure of the consumer society at home. From the Tahitian perspective it appears that the expatriate suffers from the Polynesian cultural and environmental constraints militating against change, and yet, as we shall see, an examination of the cultural history of the consumer society shows that its whole momentum is to control change and ultimately, absurdly, to attempt to defeat it. This is, in fact, only a seeming contradiction, but the synthesis of thesis and antithesis requires an examination of the origins of these expatriate needs which turn toxic in paradise.

~3~

Cargo Cults: Capturing the Intellect

Cargo cults are millennial movements that have sprung up throughout the world when isolated, primitive cultures have come into contact with radically more advanced civilizations. After a period of confusion, a prophet appears in the primitive culture who explains the wonders of the advanced civilization in terms of the natives' traditional world view, and interprets the arrival of these wonders as the signal of the dawning of a new age. Thus, after World War II, Melanesians would sometimes build airstrips, advised by their prophets that this ritual would bring about the return of the planes with their wondrous cargo.

Perhaps the most dramatic piece of evidence that consumer behavior is something more than the desire for consumer goods is offered by the cargo cult, the name given to this intriguing cultural anomaly because "cargo" is the pidgin term for all Western goods. Consider a Stone Age New Guinean the first ·time he is confronted by the arrival of a helicopter, an event unassimilable within this traditional world view. At that point, it would seem that the native has two choices. He can either try to fit the concept of the helicopter into his primitive world view, or he can abandon his culture over its failure to explain adequately the helicopter and become a disciple of the modern age. If this native is an adult, he really has only one choice, and that is to fit the helicopter into his traditional world view. This is the function of a cargo cult. In this chapter I will use the phenomenon of the cargo cult to show that the intellect plays a role in the lives of these

natives fundamentally different from what it does in the lives
of the producers and consumers of cargo.

I hope that the resonances I have described between the
expatriates and the Tahitians have prepared the way for some
of the contrasts that differentiate a consumer from a nonconsumer society. Characterizing such differences can be an
elusive and frustrating problem. For one thing, consumer
societies are a recent event, really dating only to World War II.
This means that at some point the transition between noncon-
suming and consuming societies was made. So it is necessary
not only to contrast consumer behavior longitudinally with
respect to nonconsumer behavior as it is represented in today's
world, but also historically, so that we might understand what
events marked the evolution of the consumer society. Not an
easy task, as becomes apparent from even a cursory glance at
the Babel of conceptions of consumer behavior.

In the broadest terms we think of a consumer society as one
that offers its members a wide selection of goods and services.
This broad notion is bound up with concepts of credit, with
capital, with marketing, with technological advance, and with
a second tier of connotations that suggests that the goods and
services offered make life more convenient, less laborious,
safer, more removed from the caprices of nature, and more
meaningful. The measure of a consumer society's advances is
the standard of living. Standard of living is an economic
notion, stressing material measure of status. In recent years
the stresses between the standard of living and the environmental and social costs of maintaining that standard of living
have become so obtrusive that economists like Paul
Samuelson have begun talking about a quality-of-life index
which is designed to adjust the standard of living to some of
the noneconomic costs it entails. This brings us to the other
side of the coin. The words consumer society also have
connotations of needless waste, avarice, pollution, privilege,
oligopolism, and economic conspiracy.

Then there is the consumer in that society. The word
consumer does not so much evoke an image of an affluent

beneficiary of the consumer society's cornucopia as it does the image of the helpless victim of the various frauds, price fixings, deceptive advertising campaigns, and trade conspiracies of the consumer society's corporate structure. There is a schizophrenia in the conception of the consumer society: villainous when viewed in terms of a corporate superstructure and victimized when considered in terms of its human substrate.

Common conceptions of consumer behavior are atomistic and economic. Moreover, the relationship between the consumer and the consumer society's corporate and political superstructure has been poorly articulated. Within academia, the consumer has been analyzed as an amalgam of facets. He is a set of buying patterns, social aspirations, and anxieties. There is a schizophrenia again in the studies of the consumer made by academia as opposed to those made by the advertising community. As one veteran ad man remarked, academia views the consumer as much more manipulable than he is; the advertising community fears that he is less manipulable than they might hope.

Primarily, though, when consumer behavior is discussed, the object of analysis is the American citizen wearing his hat as purchaser. The implication is that when the consumer is not wearing his hat as buyer, he is something else. For instance, he is a voter. Even though many of the same techniques used to influence purchases are used to influence votes, as a voter, the American is presumed to have much greater autonomy, and to be much less susceptible to manipulation than he is as purchaser. A person is also credited with a great deal of autonomy when it comes to individual tastes in music or art, or in the career he or she chooses. There is considerable difference of opinion about the degree of an American's rational autonomy, depending on which aspect of his behavior is being discussed and which model of human nature is used as a guide. For the behavioral psychologist, the individual has no more free will than a white rat trained to run through a maze; while for the market economist, the individual is an irascibly self-aware and autonomous entity.

To establish the consumer's identity by sorting through the variety of academic and popular notions that encrust the word would be merely to demonstrate the principle that perceptions of a given behavior reflect the properties of the lens through which the behavior is perceived. However, there is a succinct way we might investigate one of the basic characteristics of consumer behavior. That is by contrasting a given behavior in a consumer and nonconsumer society. It so happens that I have an example in mind. Let us then consider the most obtrusive and commonly perceived characteristic of consumer behavior; namely, that consumer behavior has to do with purchasing.

After all, it is the purchase that invigorates a consumer society. When we make a purchasing decision as a consumer, we mobilize resources and organize the lives of the people necessary to service our desires. The evidence upon which different notions of consumer behavior are built are the purchasing patterns of consumers. Such decisions are, so to speak, the bottom line. However, it is a mistake to assume that a particular buying pattern or interest in consumer goods is what makes a consumer. The discussion of encyclopedia sales suggested that in a consumer society the sale is not just an economic transaction, but an act that integrates the individual into the consumer society as a whole. Let us now explore buying behavior where there is no integrated system of such purchases, where the people do not have the personality structure necessary to a consumer society. I am thinking of Tahiti, and, for a more dramatic example, of New Guinea.

Earlier I noted some contrasts between the world view of the Tahitians and the world view of the expatriates who came there to live. Actually, world view is perhaps too tame an expression, because the difference is not just in the way the two groups view the world, it is evident in the way they act in the world and there is, as Martin Heiddeger noted, a difference between the two. Still, much of the confusion that revolves around the question of how much the Tahitians have changed is caused by the marked similarity between the purchasing behavior of many Tahitians and expatriates.

On the surface it would appear that many Tahitians have become consumers. Around Papeete, there are great numbers of Tahitians driving new and expensive French imported cars. Tahitians flock in abundance to department stores in Papeete and purchase many of the disposable and convenience items that are characteristic of the goods ascribed to a consumer society. Moreover, there is evidence that some Tahitians are becoming status-conscious, a prospect which is dismaying to all of us who thought we had found the one truly democratic people on earth. However, when Tahitian purchasing behavior and status-consciousness is examined more closely it becomes clear that it is premature to herald or bemoan the Tahitian transition from nonconsumer to consumer society.

For a complex variety of reasons, the French pour a great deal of money into Tahiti. Through government jobs and subsidies they have vastly inflated the amount of currency in Tahitian pockets. A receptionist working for a government ministry can earn close to $800 a month. Those Tahitians not working directly for the government benefit from a great variety of supports and subsidies. Families in the environs of Papeete benefit from the lease of their lands. In short there is a lot of money available to Tahitians, and in many cases, they do not really have to go out of their way to get it. In fact they *won't* go out of their way to get it.

Tahitians are not going to refuse money that is thrust into their hands, but it is the rare Tahitian who reorganizes his life in its pursuit. And so, with the manna from the French, they buy cars and consumer goods, but the relationship between the money and the goods is coincidental, and not part of an integrated system as it is in the United States.

Examination shows that few Tahitians have adapted themselves to fit managerial molds. Their role in the economic system is largely passive. They serve as a reluctant work force. Those who do adapt to the European mode find themselves alienated from their Tahitian neighbors. Bankers tell me that few Tahitians understand credit. Evidence of this is the rather active trade in used cars, which, I am informed, is largely supplied by repossessions. The Tahitian will buy a car, make a few payments, and then become *fi'u* with this preposterous practice of continuing to pay for something he already possesses.

Tahiti has little industry, laughable exports; the only real source of cash is the 800,000 tourists (about the number who visit Hawaii in a month) who come through the islands each year. Yet prices are astronomical, and no one seems short of cash except perhaps those few poor expatriates who struggle to maintain a foothold in the islands. Consumer behavior in Tahiti is artificial, the product of French largesse. Such transformations as have occurred in Tahiti are not the product of Tahitian efforts, but rather reflect the managerial expertise of Europeans. Consumer tastes in Tahiti are not serviced by home-based industry, but rather fuel the economies of France and the United States. Tahitian purchases mobilize resources and reorganize the lives of those necessary to service those desires, but the lives and resources affected are elsewhere. The fact that Tahitians have developed a taste for consumer goods aids the great consumer societies, but it does not mean that Tahitians have become consumers. Should the Europeans disappear, the Tahitians would not—as of 1977—be able to service these newly acquired tastes. This is not only because the islands lack resources, but also because of a fundamental difference between the relationship of the Tahitian to the world around him, and the relationship of the consumer to the world around him.

To refine some of these basic points of contrast between consumer and nonconsumer societies let us move farther westward in the Pacific and consider some people who truly love consumer goods, but who have some interesting ideas of where these goods come from and how they are produced. These people are representatives of the hundreds of tribes who live in Papua, New Guinea.

As a segment of the European expatriate population in a nonwhite country, anthropologists in New Guinea are probably a larger piece of the pie than they are in any other country on earth. However, there are probably more people in New

Guinea and neighboring West Irian who have never seen a European than there are in any other country on earth. And of those who have been exposed to European values, more New Guineans still retain their Stone Age ways than anywhere else, except perhaps West Irian. The second two sentences explain the first sentence: New Guinea is, from the anthropologists' point of view, the last great reserve of aboriginal peoples. It is also the richest country in the Pacific in resources, and the collision of the aboriginal mind and the goods and industrial might of the West, has in dozens of instances produced the bizarre but persistent phenomenon called the cargo cult. Where we see chemistry, they see alchemy. Through cargo cults, the nonconsumer mind of the New Guineans explains European wealth while protecting the integrity of the aboriginal view of the world.

When we think of New Guinea, we think of headhunters, fearsome jungles, exotic diseases, dangerous animals. Actually, nature is quite benign in New Guinea. About the only dangerous creatures on the huge island are the New Guineans themselves, who are wondrously bellicose. There are no big cats, nor big anythings except birds. There are no primates. The principal mammals are the kus kus, a golden-haired relative of the opossum, a variety of rats (regarded as a delicacy), and small kangaroos. Man imported the pig, some of whom have gone wild. There are some poisonous snakes, but not the assortment one finds in northern Queensland six hundred miles to the south. New Guinea's wildlife is mostly winged, and there is a spell-binding variety of songbirds and raptors. Still, compared with jungles of Africa, South America, and Asia, New Guinea is a mild place with not much to fear.

Both the absence of dangerous game, and the absence of other primates has had its effect on the belief systems of many of these tribes. Although there are several hundred different tribes, there are communalities that run through their world views. One communality contrasts strikingly with the evolutionary world view common to aboriginal peoples in the jungles of Africa, South America, and Malaysia, or the Plains Indians of North America. Without exposure to a grade of primates that might reinforce the links between animal and man, the New Guineans, like the fathers of Western thought, have concluded that there are no such evolutionary links. A common myth of creation in New Guinea sees man as having come from the sky world, falling into a world already populated with kus kus, cassowary, and, in a bit of tribal chauvinism, already populated with rival clans. Not exposed to large predators (with the exception of sharks which threaten coastal fishermen), or with any other animal that might challenge man's hegemony, New Guineans commonly arrive at the conclusion that the various plants and animals of their environment are a mere resource, placed at man's disposal for him to do with as he wishes. This also contrasts markedly with the mythologies of other jungle peoples who see man occupying a somewhat humbler and more threatened station in the evolutionary scheme of things.

In Enga province in the western Highlands of New Guinea, a common myth of creation has an ancestor descending to earth from the sky world. The sky world is like earth but without terrestrial calamities such as frost and mudslides. The fellow who drops in from the sky world is described as wandering around until he comes across a woman and begets a son. When the mother offers her breast to the child it seals man's terrestrial fate. It is a somewhat underdeveloped myth of the Fall, compared with the *Sturm und Drang* that accompanied our departure from Eden. However, structurally it is very similar to the Western view of man's origins, and the Enga belief that man is the epitome of creative effort with the world as his playpen also squares very nicely with our own view of things.

Later I will try to show how the ecological situation of the cradle of Western thought had its effects on our belief systems and our view of man's place in nature, and also how our view of man's place in nature in turn led to the emergence of consumer societies. For now, let us consider these Stone Age people who, in many respects, take a view of the world very similar to our own, but who are clearly not members of a consumer society.

If we consider cultures as occupying different places on a

scale that has mysticism at one extreme and materialism at the other, we would find yet another similarity between traditional New Guinean society and our own. Both of us are much closer to the materialistic end of the scale than the mystical.

Peter Lawrence, in his classic study of cargo cults, *Road Bilong Cargo,* described the religion of the coastal New Guineans of the Madang region as a "technology; which the native used to maintain his central and paramount position in the cosmic order." Their world is entirely pragmatic. If you want your yams to grow better, you perform a certain ceremony. If, as is unlikely given the bountiful climate, they then do not grow well, it is because the ceremony was improperly performed, or because of the interference of an unappeased ancestor. When not invoked, the gods disappear. Their world, says Lawrence, is an entirely physical realm with no place for the supernatural. It is "impossible to distinguish between the sphere of the natural and that of the supernatural, since gods and spirits are just as much a part of the order of nature as birds and animals."

As in Tahiti, there is no concern for eternal values. "Man's primary concern was his own welfare." Religion which blends indistinguishably with magic is a means of ensuring man's control over the plants, men, and animals of the environment. There is no reward in the next world for good works.

It should be obvious by now that New Guinea also falls into the category described by Robert Levy as a "steady-state" sociocultural milieu. And as is the case in Tahiti, the reinforcements of this steady-state are not solely evident in the ethical system, but also carry over into the New Guinean's relationship to economic and intellectual matters.

For instance, they dismiss the importance of intellectual discovery, says Lawrence, except in minor matters. Secular education is informal and unimportant; true knowledge comes through initiation to myths, rituals, and taboos. This knowledge is in turn validated in the manner of a self-fulfilling prophecy by the regularity ("monotony" is the word Lawrence uses) of social and economic life.

There is no concept of growth as we know it in our Western

society, no concept of profit, and, without notions of profit or reinvestment, no force for change. There is no specialization in village life, and, says Lawrence, the society is egalitarian and quasianarchical with each family having equal access to resources. (The situation is somewhat different in the Highlands in this regard.) "Despite the prominence of materialism," says Lawrence, "there was nothing akin to the Protestant Ethic to sanction attempts at individual economic advancement at the expense of the group."

The world of these coastal natives is at every point reduced to material terms. Relationships and alliances with other clans as well as with the ancestors are ratified in material terms. "The whole visible world," writes Lawrence, "—annually ripening crops, fertility of pigs, success in hunting—far from allowing it an aura of mysticism, proclaimed that it was solidly based on verified and empirical fact. There was no need—in fact no room—for an independent human intellect."

It is not just that there is no room for an independent human intellect, it is, as the case of expatriates in Tahiti shows, that a roving intellect poses a profound threat to a culture that seeks to maintain an orderly relationship to its ecological niche. Another threat to such order is a sense of time as objective and cumulative beyond the life of the individual. Lawrence noticed that the time frame of the New Guinean world is a constant span of several generations. With each new generation, distant forebears are forgotten. When under missionary influence natives were asked to date the birth of Christ, they would steadfastly maintain that it occurred three or four generations ago—just over the living horizon—and they would maintain this insistence through a time span of several generations! Similarly, New Guineans have no quarrel with the notion that the world was created in a few days. An anthropologist, Theodore Ahrens, notes that in the coastal regions, an hour and a half's work a day will secure a living. One plants the seeds and a few months later one harvests the crops. "For the native," says Ahrens, "the result is automatic and instantaneous." It is a creationist universe. It is also—and this is crucial if one is to understand the difference between the surface consumer behavior of New Guineans and the deeper consumer behavior of the Westerner—a world without progress. There is no sense of cumulative advance from a benighted past.

Given such predispositions, one would imagine that the New Guinea natives would have been a perfect field in which missionaries might sow their seeds. Here was a population predisposed to believing the myth of creation, and sharing similar views of man's place in nature to those outlined in Genesis. In fact, in many cases missionaries found themselves the most popular people in town. Services would be packed, and not a member of the congregation would be asleep. But throughout the Madang region at different times over the last 150 years, and throughout New Guinea as well, the message delivered by the missionaries was not the one the parishioners received. It is a delicious irony that missionaries preaching abstinence and self-denial should be perceived solely as the possessors of the secrets of prosperity and indulgence. For in many different cases the missionaries were looked upon as guardians of the secret rituals through which the Europeans got the ancestors to deliver cargo.

Cargo cults are not unique to New Guinea. They have occurred throughout Melanesia and Polynesia, and, in medieval times, in Europe. Cargo cults represent an attempt by a culture to integrate into an existing belief system or world view the disorienting experience of exposure to novel technologies and peoples. I use the word world view because some cargo cults in New Guinea demonstrate a willingness to sacrifice the details of a belief system, if that serves to maintain the structure of the native's relationship to his environment. Cargo cults serve a defensive function: they throw up an explanation of events that overwhelm or contradict the capacities of the traditional culture, and, in so doing, attempt to preserve the foundations of the native's world. Perhaps nowhere on earth has the confrontation between traditional and alien been more dramatic than in the case of New Guinean exposure to Europeans. However, the elastic powers of traditional New Guinean culture has proved equal to the challenge of the Space Age, perhaps largely because of the many similarities that relate the world views of the Stone Age natives and the Space Age Europeans.

Cargo cults are a much more common phenomenon in New Guinea than is evident from a perusal of the literature. Peter Lawrence studied five successive cargo cults that sprang up in the coastal region of Madang in the period from the turn of the century to the 1950s. Other anthropologists, such as Worsely, Berendt, Burridge, Ingliss, and Salisbury, have examined other cargo cults, but the breadth of the phenomenon is hard to imagine. Cargo cults still regularly appear today as commercial interests, anthropologists, and voluntary agencies push their way into remote areas of the provinces. While I was in New Guinea, I heard of two anthropologists who had recently had cargo-cult activity coalesce around their presence in villages, and Theodore Ahrens went so far as to say, "I have yet to meet the New Guinean who has abandoned the underpinnings of his cargo belief." Since the underpinnings of cargoistic activity are the traditional world view, this statement is not so dramatic as it seems at first. The breadth of the predisposition to cargo beliefs became apparent in 1975, when, just before independence, there was the widespread feeling that all European property (and according to some, the secrets of the cargo ritual that produced that property) would be returned to the New Guineans with independence.

This feeling, although not a proper cargo belief, illustrates the common properties of cargo cults. They are often millennial movements. The arrival of Europeans is interpreted by a native prophet to mean that release from earthly toil and strife is at hand. All who follow the prophet (who is the possessor of the rituals the Europeans use to produce cargo) will be rewarded when the cargo is returned to the New Guineans, its rightful owners, who earlier forfeited their rights to cargo, in some cases through stupidity, and in others through treachery. The idea that Europeans possess cargo through treachery or duplicity runs through many cargo beliefs, and also accounts for the European notion that cargo cults are a threatening phenomenon to be suppressed wherever they occur. They are disruptive to New Guineans as well, because in some cases the natives, anticipating the millennium, will abandon their crops and await the arrival of the cargo.

In the five cargo beliefs Lawrence studied there is an amusing progression in the role Europeans play in these beliefs. At first contact in the Madang region, Europeans were perceived as deities, first indigenous deities, then, after exposure to Germans, as hostile deities. However, after a little more exposure to the stumbling, sweating, tenderfooted, slow-witted Europeans, who seemed to have difficulty learning native dialects, the natives decided that Europeans did not really live up to the behavior the tribes expected of a deity, and came to the conclusion that Europeans were human. Because Europeans were so manifestly stupid, the natives decided that European wealth could not derive from European resourcefulness, but rather must have been stolen.

This brings us back to the point of this consideration of cargo activity—namely that surface consumer behavior does not constitute a consumer society, and more particularly, purchasing behavior alone is inadequate to understand a consumer society. The New Guineans, after all, were delighted with the appearance of consumer goods. Many of the missionaries and administrators who came in contact with cargo-cult activity were supremely shocked by its occurrence because they had been previously led to believe by transformations in the surface behavior of the natives that the natives were happily adapting themselves to modern ways. For instance, one cargo leader, Yali, had been a model soldier during the Second World War, and had been chosen for a variety of administrative and liaison duties because of the seeming wholeheartedness of his adoption of modern ways. He had even had exposure to modern industry in Australia. We will get back to Yali; for the moment let us consider the one "Christian" cargo belief in the Madang region. This was the case referred to earlier in which the missionaries believed that they had had astounding success in conversions and church attendance, only to be confronted with the bewildering truth that the natives perceived Christianity solely as a road to the luxurious, slothful, work-free life enjoyed by the Europeans.

Lawrence points out that the natives never associated the production of cargo with work because they never saw Europeans working. Rather, they observed huge cargo ships arrive and disgorge supplies that bore no visible connection to the endeavors of the Europeans around them. Moreover, the Europeans would celebrate the arrival of these ships, reinforcing the belief that cargo had a miraculous origin.

The natives had no trouble envisioning heaven, but rationalizing the relationship between their indigenous deities and the Trinity did pose some epistemological problems. Lawrence notes how the missionaries, in their zeal to win converts to Christianity, actually abetted the conversion of Christianity into paganism:

> Both Lutherans and Catholics, whether strict or permissive in their demands on their baptized converts, seem to have been unaware of the principles underlying local pagan ritual, and therefore failed to convince the people of its futility. They left them with the impression that they acknowledged the existence of the traditional deities. For a start, the Catholic practice of claiming to neutralize dangerous gods with holy water was tantamount to recognition of their power. Moreover, even when both Lutherans and Catholics denounced polygyny and sorcery, and the Lutherans other forms of ritual as well, they did not go beyond describing them as satanic, *samting bilong Satan*. The natives interpreted this phrase in characteristically concrete terms. Virtually all their secular and sacred customs, especially their secret ritual formulae, were believed to have been given them by their gods and goddesses. Hence, if these customs came from Satan, it followed that the old deities were themselves "satans." They were identified with the Devil of official Christianity and, like the Devil, were assumed to have been brought into being by God himself, who had also enabled them to create the New Guinea material culture. This was neatly incorporated in the general doctrine of the Third Cargo Belief. It was said that when Ham came to New Guinea, God gave him and his descendants control over the "satans" so that some sort of economic and social existence would be possible. Thus the

pagan gods, far from passing into oblivion, were still accepted as real and powerful in their original spheres.

... Superficially, the natives had been converted to Christian monotheism, but, in reality, they were still thinking and acting in terms of polytheism.

Lawrence in other cases goes on to elaborate the many compatibilities between the native and Christian world view that facilitated this polytheistic embrace of Christianity. We have covered some of them: both Christian and native live in a creationist universe, both see man as the pinnacle of creation on earth, neither sees any evolutionary relationship between man and the rest of nature; and we have introduced other elements of similarity: for instance, the similar ecological situation of New Guinea and the cradle of monotheism where both lacked large predators and primates that might temper man's judgment on his place in the natural order. Yet despite these similarities, examples such as the third cargo belief and the continuing proliferation of cargo activity indicate that natives and Europeans foist entirely different organization on the same perceptual material.

Moreover, this persistence in using magico-religio explanations has survived years of attempts to persuade the natives of cargo's true origins. I heard about one anthropologist who, noticing that villagers were beginning to mythify his presence in the Goroka area, decided to short-circuit the development of any cargo cult by taking one of the more sensible village elders and explaining the material origins of European factories and electricity. He took this native to see a hydroelectric dam. Of course, this attempt to demythify cargo completely backfired, for when this native saw the immense scale of a hydroelectric dam, all his doubts about the miraculous origins of cargo vanished—he was now absolutely convinced that no human could construct something that big. The same is true for Yali, that supremely sophisticated sergeant major who so disappointed Australian administrators by turning to cargo beliefs after having been touted as a native paragon of upward mobility. During his army training, Yali visited a factory where

he was shown the industrial process that lay behind the
production of goods. Later Yali would say that he saw cargo
being produced, but that he was not shown the rear room
behind the factory where the ancestors directed the operation.

What is striking about cargo beliefs in New Guinea is that
this misunderstanding persists despite the ostensible communality of interests of Europeans and natives there. New
Guinea is not like many other aboriginal areas where natives
conscientiously eschew consumer enticements. No, in New
Guinea, most natives see consumer goods as an unqualified
good, and, as noted, view the life enjoyed by Europeans as
heaven. If a primary function of cargo-cult beliefs is to defend
the authority of a world view by assimilating into a structure
the novel experiences posed by European culture, then that
threat must be perceived unconsciously, because consciously
the natives wholeheartedly endorse any culture that will bring
them cargo.

What is the nature of the threat posed by the novelties of
European material culture to primitive culture? As should be
clear from the above précis of the third cargo belief, the
natives will willingly sacrifice details, such as ceremonies and
rituals, in the face of a more potent magic. What is preserved
through cargo ritual is a magico-religio explanation of material
phenomena as opposed to a rationalistic one. Or as J. K.
McCarthy says in his foreword to Lawrence's book, "the
'Submarine Men' of Kokopa—a cult that had its genesis in the
cargo-cult belief—is an example of how a group, sophisticated
and economically well off, preferred magical and religious
ritual to the white man's ways in their endeavor to find
betterment."

At this point there is another question which ought to be
asked: namely, what purpose does the preservation of a
magico-religio explanation of phenomena serve? For one
thing it preserves the set of relationships between the individual, the supernatural, and the material world that constitute
the native's personality. But to look a little deeper beneath the
surface, the magico-religio explanation of novel phenomena
preserves a relationship between reason and the unconscious

that becomes profoundly threatened when the novel events and rationalistic explanations are offered by Europeans. This is where differences of perceptual organization become apparent. For the natives to understand cargo as the European understands it would demand a restructuring of the role of reason in the native's personality, and in the cultural life of the community as a whole.

In describing the cultural substrate that produced cargo beliefs Lawrence notes the relatively low priorities accorded secular knowledge and individual enterprise during the rather informal education of the young. Things happen because of the intercession of a host of animistic embodiments of natural processes and forces and not because of the ingenuity or determination of men. Lawrence also pointed out the lack of specialization, the absence of concepts of growth or reinvestment, and the truncated sense of time that characterized the economic and epistemological universe of the natives. It is a world in which reason operates in strict confinement. There is nothing to prepare or even allow the native to believe that the wonders of European material culture result from the operations of intellect. His consequent decision that cargo has miraculous origins is not irrational, but highly rational given that this explanation follows the logic of a universe that hitherto has been daily ratified by experience. This relationship between reason and culture provides one point of departure from which Western man has diverged during the evolution that led to the emergence of consumer behavior. Through a consideration of this relationship we can see how we might be rational and irrational at the same time.

There is a marvelous relationship between the culture and the individual that occurs often in New Guinean society. For instance, as I have pointed out again and again, most natives greet the novelties of the consumer society with unqualified delight. Moreover, if one suddenly equipped a tribe to actually realize their hunting and aggressive ambitions, New Guinea would be shortly denuded of people, flora, and fauna. The restraints that maintain a balance between the people and their neighbors and the people and their environment are not conscious, but unconscious. Writing about the Maring in the Highlands, anthropologist Marvin Harris describes a seven-year cycle of infanticide, warfare, and pig slaughter, the whole of which, Harris says, amounts to a "trick" perpetrated on the natives by their "ancestors" to the end of maintaining environmental harmony. Their culture embodied by the do's and don't's of the "ancestors" uses the appetites and fears of the Maring to trick them into behaving in such a way that they do not overtax the reconstitutive powers of the jungle canopy. Harris's use of the word "trick" to describe the relationship between the culture (and its long-term ambitions) and the individual (with his potentially unruly appetites and aggressions) is also quite apt when applied to the relationship between cargo beliefs and their congregation.

In the unspecialized life of the village, the culture is such a close mapping of the individual personality of the native that the line between individual and group tends to blur. One woman anthropologist wrote in a report to the administrator of Enga province that should a villager see an enemy from a neighboring clan against whom the village harbors an unrequited grudge, the villager will want to kill the enemy on the spot, instantly. This woman was writing to explain a murder that took place on a runway at the local airport. She used the word "salivate" to describe the urgency and immediacy of the desire to attack the enemy clansman. I hesitate to believe that the response is quite so Pavlovian, but the exaggeration does suggest the integration of individual and collective behavior. It's a "trick" which I'm sure is the dream of every officer who had to explain to his troops why so and so was the enemy.

This relationship of an individual to his culture is only permitted by the regularity of village life. In this steady-state sociocultural milieu, the tensions defining the personality are so commonly shared and commonly defined that they take on a collective life of their own as the myths of the community. Rather than being experienced individually, aspects of this aboriginal personality are projected onto the world at large and are experienced as external events instead of subjective problems. Thus the individual personality is somewhat free of internal controls over behavior, such as pangs of conscience. Controls are in the real world and they are not intellectual but behavioral. This is the point that Levy was making about the Tahitian community. Its relevance here is that to consider only the expressed desires of the native is to get an incomplete picture of his personality, because a part of that personality is tied to his culturally shared reactions to different situations. Separated from those constraints he may appear an exceedingly unruly character, but when his behavior is viewed from the perspective of his total *effects* upon his cultural and physical ecosystem, we see a much more moderate individual. The villager's personality cannot be separated from community life. This is a point which, as we saw in the example of expatriates in Tahiti, also applies to a degree to villagers in communities like Beverly Hills and Darien.

If we interpret these cultural constraints on behavior— Harris's "trick"—to be a part of the native's personality, it becomes clear that the trick is played on one part of the native's personality by another; it is one part of the native controlling another. In the case of the natives' interpretation of cargo, the trick is at the level of the New Guinean's categorization of the novelties of European culture. The natives easily develop a working understanding of how to use the products of Western technology; however, the native is "tricked" as to the equipment's origins—a circumstance which has had negative and residual effects on the life of machinery in many parts of New Guinea. The purpose of the "ancestors'" trick on the Maring of the Highlands is to preserve the forest cover. The purpose of the cargo belief's trick is to preserve the native's world view, and ultimately to preserve a relationship between reason and the unconscious. Like Kaspar Hauser, who was isolated by a jealous king so that he might never know his power and usurp the king's throne, reason must be duped when confronted by its technological kingdom so that it does not recognize its power.

Reason's role is channeled through the narrowest possible corridors. Contrary to the case of expatriates in Polynesia, where reason mediates virtually all relationships to the islands and reorganizes the expatriate's life in its service, in New Guinea, reason's role, as the example of cargo cults illustrates, is satellite to the native's experience and understanding of his world. What is clear is that the human intellect plays a fundamentally different role in the interpretation of experience in aboriginal New Guinean culture and in the culture of European consumer societies.

It is at the level of these roles that the differences between consumer and nonconsumer societies begin to appear. While it is clear that as long as an outside agency supplies the money and the goods, the natives of New Guinea in the aboriginal state will demonstrate buying behavior that might seem to be consumer behavior. But it is my contention that as long as the structure of the native's world view remains intact—as it does in the case of cargo cults—cultural constraints will continue to maintain a relationship between the native and the environment that is conserving. As long as the natives still believe in a world influenced by the "ancestors," nature is still in charge and the role of reason is subordinated. What this means is that with the withdrawal of artificial supplies of money and goods, nature, through the authority and tricks of the ancestors, will ultimately reestablish some controls over the behavior of the natives.

What I have been trying to do is to suggest that consumer behavior is bound up with a way of looking at and relating to the world. To understand the contrast between consumer and nonconsumer behavior at its most extreme, envision a group of natives and a group of Europeans dropped into some uninhabited island in the Pacific. The difference between them would be that the constraints of the environment would ultimately organize the behavior and livelihood of the native group, while on the other hand, in the case of our consumer refugees, the impact of reason upon the behavior of the Europeans and the ecology of the area would be more apparent. On the behavioral level this impact would be evident in a much more flexible intervention in response to the problems of survival on the island.

This chapter opened with the question of whether the preference for and purchase of consumer goods was sufficient to establish that a society was a consumer society. I have used the examples of Tahitian buying behavior and cargo cults in New Guinea to suggest that it is misleading to consider buying behavior and individual desire for consumer goods as indicators of a consumer society. Moreover, the example of New Guinean cargo cults also makes it clear that materialism does not make a society a consumer society. Consumer behavior is not something the consumer can abandon by removing himself to a nonconsumer society; nor is it something that the nonconsumer can acquire by merely developing a taste for and access to consumer goods. Rather, consumer behavior is a relationship to the world that surfaces in noneconomic, as well as economic ways. At first my attempt to use expatriate malaise and cargo-cult activity as evidence in an attempt to define consumer behavior may seem stretched or arbitrary. However, the restriction of the discussion so far has been purposeful. I have implied that the level at which the difference between consumer and nonconsumer behavior becomes apparent is that of perceptual and behavioral organization, a level far more profound than the level of surface economic activity at which consumer behavior is most often studied.

This was also my earlier intent when I looked at the dynamic of a door-to-door encyclopedia sale and suggested that beneath the surface of this seemingly innocuous transaction is a complicated interaction which fuses the economic and cultural sides of life in a consumer society. We might for a moment contrast the consumer appetites described in Chapter One with those evident in cargo cults.

It would seem at first that there are remarkable similarities between consumer purchases in New Guinea and the United States. The natives buy goods with considerations of status in mind as often as they buy them for utility. This is the obvious implication of the native habit of displaying a totally wrecked vehicle in the front yard as testimony to their buying power. Moreover, in both the case of the consumer and New Guinean native, the individual is "tricked" by his culture into behaviors culturally selected.

The fundamental differences in these two cultures appears

when we consider the purposes of these two tricks. I included the example of cargo-cult behavior to suggest that the trick in that case served to camouflage the origins of consumer goods and in so doing preserve the hegemony of the "gods" as the final authority over the native's behavior. The trick in this case is on reason. Through cargo cult the native culture attempts to maintain strict proscriptions on the role of the intellect in the native's life. In a consumer decision, exactly the opposite situation prevails. As we shall see, each consumer decision *enhances* the power of reason as an influence in our daily lives.

Cargo-cult activity preserves the structure of the natives' universe. It insures that even though the natives might develop a taste for consumer goods, they are not equipped to produce them. On the other hand, the motive power behind the consumer decision in a consumer society is a reservoir of anxieties that is born of a fundamentally different relationship between reason and the unconscious. As I will try to show, the consumer decision is a device by which reason *domesticates* disenfranchised and potentially unruly unconscious forces and uses them for its own purposes.

All other differences between a consumer society and the growthless, steady-state society of New Guinea derive from this fundamental difference. The structure of personality that gives us our appetite for consumer goods also permits us to make them. The existence of a consumer society is a question not just of demand, but also of supply.

~ *PART II* ~

The Pursuit of Certainty:
Antecedents of Consumer Behavior

Part II traces the antecedents of consumer behavior to a primary conflict in human nature. It advances the idea that modern man is a proxy in what is really an evolutionary battle.

~ 4 ~

Autochthony and Evolution

I have been attempting to describe broadly certain dissonances which surface in the comparison of roles played by the intellect in the lives of Americans and in the lives of Polynesians and Melanesians. My suggestion, hardly novel, is that the intellect impinges more upon the behavior of people coming out of a modern technological society than it does upon the behavior of peoples in a near-aboriginal state. Nor is it surprising to suggest that the success of Western man is traceable to his flexibility when compared to the tradition-bound aborigine, or our more context-bound fellow creatures. However, it is becoming clear that in the West, the flexibility that has given us such an advantage over the rest of nature and more primitive societies is the very property that most clouds the prospects for our continued survival. The enhancement of the role of reason in our lives has increased the flexibility of our response to environmental challenges. Reason in the lives of Western man is a Promethean fire that has gotten out of control. This image contrasts with our self-image of autonomy and judiciousness. Moreover, the advances in science and technology, which we have interpreted as the *goal* of evolution, are actually side effects of an evolutionary battle which, as the next few chapters will show, in turn had its origins in accident. When we understand the evolutionary and cultural roots of the dissonances considered in the opening chapters, we will understand the roots of our affluence and the role of consumer behavior in the evolutionary battle being played out in man. The key to it all is the role of the intellect in human behavior.

The following chapters will attempt to make evolutionary sense out of this Promethean brush fire. Try to imagine yourself transported back in time a hundred thousand years. What would we see in human behavior that would lead us to explain the difference between man as he was then and the other great apes? What would we see twenty thousand years ago? Five thousand years ago? Now? Should we be able to contrast our findings of five thousand years ago with our findings of today, we would notice insignificant differences between the structure of the brain of our forebears and our own, but an extraordinary difference in the impact of these two groups upon the earth. We would also notice that while one particular group of present-day *homo sapiens* behave in marked contrast to their forebears, contemporaries of this group—the tribes of New Guinea for instance—behave much the way their ancestors did five thousand years ago. Finally, we would see that it was possible to bring a member of the unchanged group into the fold of the most changed in one lifetime. If it can happen in one lifetime, then why did it take five thousand years, and why did these changes occur only for some *homo sapiens* and not for all? In summary we would want to know how consumer behavior differs from that of other men and other hominoids, we would want to know how profound those differences were, when they began, and where they are leading. To answer those questions we have to go back to our beginnings.

I should say at this point that although it may seem a bit far afield to go back to the dawn of human evolution to find the roots of consumer behavior, I feel strongly that it is at these origins that the evolutionary conflict that eventually led to the development of consumer societies is most palpable. It was my interest in exploring this conflict that prompted me to write my first book, *Apes, Men, and Language*. What we find when we explore the roots of our propositional abilities is that nature does seem to have an interest in controlling reason, just as "reason" seems to have an interest in expanding its hegemony. This conflict, which has been played out on various levels during the course of human evolution, contains the key to understanding the emergence of consumer societies. First, let us briefly review the events in science that permit us to make judgments on the roots of this conflict. Then I will introduce the players in this conflict: Reason and Nature.

It would seem that there are many different kinds of evidence that might be used to hypothesize an evolutionary history of a behavior. For instance, there is evidence supplied by paleontology, by the study of homologous behaviors in related species, or by the study of dysfunctions of particular behaviors. Ultimately, however, the device that permits the interpretation of such pieces of evidence is a model that in effect gives scientific credibility to anthropocentrism. This is Haeckel's dictum known to every college sophomore: *Ontogeny recapitulates phylogeny*. This formidable collection of syllables means simply that the history of the individual repeats the history of the species. This dictum, formulated in 1866, permits us to construct an organism's phylogenetic tree. It is based upon the assumption that evolution is an accretive process. The lessons of survival are encoded successively, so that the previous states of a creature's history do not disappear but instead are superseded. Haeckel proposed that an organism retraces its evolutionary history as it develops from zygote through infancy. In effect, Haeckel suggests that as we mature in the womb, we retrace the history of the planet as experienced by our antecedents. This does not mean that at some point in our evolution we were helpless creatures whose heads were almost as big as our bodies, but it does permit us to make judgments, on the basis of various embryonic stages as well as by means of blood hemoglobins, proteins, and (more recently) electroencephalographs, regarding the closeness of our relationships to our contemporaries among the apes, and the likely shape of our forebears.

While establishing the history of an anatomical characteristic is accepted practice, the question of the evolutionary history of a behavior is much more charged and controversial. Haeckel was not referring to behavior when he formulated his dictum. However, once we accept that there is a biological substrate to behavior, it follows that the accretive process that is recapitulated during the ontogeny of the individual's physical characteristics will also be replicated during the development of its behavioral repertoire. Eventually this idea seeped through science as well. Initially there was great resistance to the idea that man's nobility was an accident of the same forces that produced the rat. Man's behavior was ultimately responsible to reason while animals were little more than automata filling out nature's design. To assume a common perspective for the study of both animal and human behavior was to question the very foundation of Western man's self-image. But this was the foundation of ethology, which assumes that regardless of which side of the animal / human line one examines, there is a biological regularity to particular behavior just as there is a biological regularity to that creature's bone structure and physical characteristics. Thus, ethology gives us a perspective to compare behavioral homologies across species, while Haeckel's dictum offers a guide to interpreting such behavioral homologies that occur during ontogeny.

From an evolutionary perspective, the hallmark of human adaptiveness is man's flexibility. Not only can we adapt to extremes of the world's climate, we can also adapt to radical environmental changes within one generation. There are other creatures—the (ahem) cockroach and the rat for example—that are also very adaptable, but the characteristic of our adaptiveness is the way in which we rework the world to conform to our needs. We are able to turn psychic energy into physical advantage, or, because psychic energy is ultimately physical energy, it might be better to say that we are able to gain enormous physical leverage out of that relatively small amount of energy that goes into enabling propositional thought. This, at least, is the cost-benefit analysis made by nature during human evolution. Neurologist Norman Geshwind has noted that from nature's point of view the human brain is a terribly expensive piece of equipment. It gobbles up a quarter of cardiac output, which means that there is a direct trade-off between the brain and the muscles (something that anyone who has ever "choked" while playing tennis will know immediately). For this reason it is unlikely that any animal, including man, has more brain than it uses. It also means that the enhancement of the role of the intellect in our adaptive strategy tended to be self-reinforcing: as we deepened our reliance on the intellect we lessened our ability to respond otherwise to environmental challenges which, in turn, further focused pressure on the brain as a means of adapting and surviving. In nature, as in economics, there is no such thing as a free lunch. Let us briefly look at the origins of this pattern of adaptation. Actually there is an anomaly which offers a dramatic new perspective on the origins of thought.

The following suppositions about the origins and nature of propositional thought have been partly shaped by the study of homologous behaviors in apes. For the past ten years experimenters have been successfully teaching languages to chimpanzees and gorillas. Apart from the awesome implications these experiments have with regard to our notions of the uniqueness of human behavior (considered at length in my book *Apes, Men, and Language*), language-like behavior in these close relatives offers homologies through which we might understand the origins as well as the nature of our own language and propositional abilities. Allen and Beatrice Gardner, two comparative psychologists, were able to teach chimp Washoe a gestural language where all previous attempts to teach chimps spoken language had foundered. A young female gorilla named Koko now has a sign-language vocabulary approaching five hundred words. On the other hand, in experiments attempting to teach apes spoken language, no animal learned to utter more than eight words. Moreover, there is ample evidence that the great apes use this gestural language spontaneously and productively in many of the ways we use spoken language. Chimps and gorillas have used the language to swear, to describe novel situations, to express emotions, and to lie. They have made up words, they have linked words metaphorically, and they have used the language to refer to past events. Yet they cannot talk. What does this tell us?

It tells us that were the proverbial Martian biologist to visit earth to study the great apes—man included—he might find the points of similarity between ape and human behavior as interesting as the differences. There is no question that he would note the staggering contrasts that marked the *impact* humans had upon the earth, but in seeking to account for that impact, he would note that for the bulk of the four billion naked apes, there was but a small percentage of their behavior that contrasted markedly with that of the other great apes. Had our Martian friend taken this survey five thousand years ago, he would have been hard pressed to really measure the difference in impact between man and ape. In order to explain the dramatic events of the last five thousand—and even fifty—years, we have to go back five hundred thousand years. Again, it is that small percentage of our behavior that I hope to isolate. Because something got out of hand recently in human evolution which has enabled us to utterly rework the face of the earth.

The use of sign language by apes gives us the opportunity to observe some of the problems nature had to solve in order to equip us for propositional communication and tool-making. That problem basically is: How do you equip an animal to rapidly modify its behavior without throwing into disequilibrium its entire behavioral program for survival? The answer to the problem, as evident in the abilities of apes, is that you tap and enhance a preexisting ability, and that you strictly control the animal's latitude in the modifications it might make on its behavior. You do this by controlling the animal's access to its propositional abilities, and you do this—literally—by keeping its hands busy with other things. Jane Goodall has observed chimps stripping stalks to fashion a rudimentary tool to fish for termites. Such a series of actions is a type of proposition. The act of stripping a stalk has no direct connection with the act of picking up a termite and eating it. Instead, the connection between the two events is built upon the chimp's analysis and solution to the problem presented by the small apertures that allow entrance to a termite mound. It is the kind of insight that Wolfgang Köhler, the father of Gestalt psychology, noticed in a captive chimp named Sultan, who in a flash of brilliance attached two sticks together in order to get at some bananas that were out of reach.

Let us examine the radical events these actions signal. To build its tool, the chimp had to organize a series of movements, and it had to fashion an extrasomatic implement to compensate for physical limitations. The solution of the problem demands propositional control of the hands, which in turn demands the existence of a time-space framework separate from the ongoing continuum of stimulus and response. Essentially, to solve this problem, the chimp has to be able to *abstract* itself from the busy details of living. It needs to be able to abstract from the mass of sense data the attributes of the world and their laws of organization, if it is going to have something to work with while abstracted from the moment. Finally it needs some psychic space where it can pool the refined products of this sense data and which it can then furnish with the resulting abstractions and experiment. Any organism that can associate a stimulus with a response can "learn," but the order of conceptual organization required for an animal to fashion a tool in order to achieve a desired end requires that the animal be equipped to play God. It must become shaper of its own behavior; it must preempt nature's function to some small degree. It must be able to adapt and control the movements of its hands, not solely according to the inherited lessons of evolution, but also in response to its own analytical conclusions. This was the fire given to Prometheus, but as we shall see, just as nature equipped man to overrule our "natural" inclinations, so did nature attempt to control which areas these usurpations might affect. It is in this conflict that the origins of modern alienation and consumer behavior lie.

The anatomical revisions that permit the animal to construct and have access to a surrogate world in which it might work out propositions are associated with connections in the brain that permit information to get from one part of the neocortex to another without being channeled through subcortical structures. In order to construct a symbol one has to be able to associate information coming from, for instance, the visual-haptic channel with information received through the auditory mode. This is called cross-modal transfer, and previous to the experiments with sign language and apes, it was thought that apes could not affect such transfers because incoming sense information was mediated by the limbic system, a subcortical structure which is a type of clearing house in which information is channeled to be acted on and interpreted in accordance with the animals' genetic behavioral heritage. The image is of the apes pinned to a visceral level of response to incoming information. Quite simply, if all incoming information is given an emotional charge and is administered as an instruction to act, it cannot simultaneously be pooled with other sense data and analyzed. In effect, analysis demands that selected information not be acted on by the administrative centers of the brain, and this requires anatomical revisions, neural spikes, that interconnect different areas of the neocortex while bypassing the action centers of the mid-brain. Analytical abilities exist in *tension* with the genetically encoded lessons of evolution. For information to be processed and acted on by the analytical modality requires the suppression or bypassing of its interpretation by those parts of the brain that interpret such information in accordance with our innate structures of response.

This is the difference between "learning" by associating a stimulus with a reward, and learning to shape behavior propositionally to achieve some end. The first requires only a basic set of sensitivities, the second requires anatomical restructurings. What I want to show in the next few pages is that in the first painful steps of human evolution, nature began to lose her hold over our propositional abilities, although she did not lose her hold over these abilities in other animals. Early in our evolution, the enhancement of our propositional abilities and nature's attempts to ensure their proper use took on the properties of a power struggle. This section will show the origins of this struggle and suggest that there is legitimate cause to personify the combatants in this power struggle. It is essential that the nature of this struggle be understood if we are to understand the role consumer societies play in this continuing drama.

We might imagine a point in man's evolution when his tool-making consisted of the fashioning of termite-fishing twigs. Little complexity would be necessary in the symbolic system needed to form these rudimentary propositions because such a system would demand only the most limited displacement from the moment. There are numerous scenarios that might explain why chimps have remained chimps while our analytical abilities ballooned wildly, but the scenario I find most plausible is that man was an unsuccessful competitor within the rain forest, and found himself pushed through a variety of changing environments, changes that placed great selective pressure for flexibility in man's relatively plastic hands and that also placed great demands on nascent analytical abilities. But, as I pointed out earlier, the reliance on analytical abilities to solve environmental challenges tends to be self-reinforcing, because both the figurative and literal displacement from immediate response that this entails can only erode the crispness of the animal's genetic competitive edge in its ecological niche, which in turn demands increased propositional intervention. As our reliance on these abilities deepened, increased displacement from stimuli in time and space (especially if we were adapting to a changing environment) meant that immediate reference to actual objects became more difficult, and this required a more elaborately furnished, displaced world. The environmental pressures were toward the creation of a surrogate world which would exist as an enduring metaphor in the brain. This surrogate world would be our blackboard on which we might work out strategies for survival. It would be furnished with symbols that were analogs of objects in our ancestors' environment, and we might imagine that the repertoire of symbols directly followed from the importance of their referents to our survival. It is no accident that Eskimos have eleven different words for snow.

This surrogate world needs not only analogs for the objects of the environment, it also needs a set of principles that replicate the relationships that govern those symbols. Symbol and logic as well as word and grammatical principles probably all share a common origin, since originally a symbol might only be understood in its relationships with other objects. At the level of original analysis, symbol and logic are inextricably bound, just as a chimp's understanding of the manipulations that turn a twig into a tool were originally bound to the twig it was manipulating. We might imagine that before a chimp learned to fashion a twig for termite fishing, it would stick a twig into a termite mound until some feature of the twig prevented it from being pushed in farther. Then followed a stage in which chimps would shape the tool as it was pushed into the mound. Ultimately, the chimps analyzed those attributes of the twig and helped or impeded their use as tools, which allowed the chimp to fashion the tools before attempting to use them.

In the chimp's manipulations of a twig to create a tool, we can also infer a common origin for language and technology. For instance, if the chimp or hominid performed the series of actions that characterize stripping the twig, without the twig in its hands, it would be constructing a sentence (provided there was a symbol for the twig) describing that manipulation. Thus, the same programmed series of actions constitutes both the source of the logic of a proposition, a schematic for a technological intervention, and the grammar of the sentence describing that proposition.

Anthropologist Gordon Hewes, one of the foremost proponents of the gestural theory of language origins, believes that this ordinal ability to program motor actions may be the "deep structure" of syntax. This argument suggests that man first learned propositional communication through gestures, and that later, a concatenation of pressures led to the transfer to vocal speech. Hewes notes that similar damage to the brain can upset a person's ability to put together both actions in a series and words in sentences. He writes:

Neither tool-using actions nor words, whether gestural or vocal, normally appear as isolated bits of behavior. Instead they are components of more complex programs of action. Such programs can be disorganized or destroyed in cases of damage to the brain and the disturbances of language are remarkably similar to those in motor skills. Some forms of aphasia are syntactical—the patient can still produce words, or recognize them, but cannot combine them into meaningful sentences, just as some forms of apraxia exhibit a deficit in programming sequences of meaningful action, rather than isolated motor acts such as reaching or holding. The condition known as ideomotor apraxia . . . suggests a disturbance in an underlying deep structure very similar to that which makes propositional language possible. Both motor-skill sequences and sentence constructions are adversely affected by the same lesion in many instances. It could be that this fundamental capacity to acquire and utilize complex patterned sequences, expressible in tool-manipulation, in gesture-language, and later in speech, is the "deep structure" Chomsky really should have been writing about, and that in the long course of hominization, it is the evolutionary growth of this kind of syntactic capacity that has been so important, and not its separate manifestations in technology and language.

Let us momentarily get back to our Martian friend who is attempting to isolate what differentiates our impact on the earth from that of the other great apes. Should he contrast the technologies of man and apes, the communication systems of man and apes, and the social organization or management capabilities of man and apes, he might trace these tributaries back to their source and notice that in each case abilities present in apes are greatly exaggerated in man, and that each of these spheres of behavior rests on the ability to construct and express complex patterned sequences. Moreover, he would see that the source of each innovation introduced through these patterned sequences ultimately involves an experimental simulation.

What I am concerned with here, however, are some of the constraints that appear to affect the chimp's use of sign language, and the principal constraint that has so far become apparent is a limitation affecting what we might call the chimp's concentration. In *Apes, Men, and Language*, I used the word *displacement* to refer to this ability to ignore the pressing demands of the moment in pursuit of the solution to some problem. What I am referring to in both cases is an ability to shift from what might be called an action modality into a propositional modality. In the case of sign language and tool-making, this involves control over the use of the hands. I use the word modality because, as I have argued earlier, sense information is interpreted, and even routed differently in the brain, when it is used propositionally, rather than simply acted on or stored. When we think about a problem or communicate through language, we shift (for those parts of the communication that are propositional) into a modality in which thinking *occurs*. Whether this thinking is in the form of hearing voices out in the jungle or brainstorming in a conference room is immaterial. What matters from the point of view of our evolutionary impact on the world is that we have recourse to this modality, which is abstracted from the flux of the moment.

Chimp, gorilla, and orang have recourse to this modality as well, but their access is somewhat more limited. The difference between man and ape brings to mind the Greek word *autochthonous,* which means "sprung from the earth," deriving as it does from *autos* (self) and *chthon* (earth). It is used occasionally to describe the heroic because of its suggestion of the arduous wresting of authority from nature that characterizes those who seek to control their destiny. It might well serve as a metaphor for the relationship between the propositional and natural modalities of behavior. The chimp and gorilla are proportionately more chthonic than we are.

During a survey of many chimp utterances, I noticed that while their vocabularies increased according to the efforts of their instructors, attempts to increase the length of chimp utterance has not grown proportionately to vocabulary size. The length of the chimp's communicative pulses are rarely more than eight signs. A chimp with a sixty-word vocabulary uses combinations of about the length and complexity of a chimp with a much larger vocabulary.

I interpret this circumstance in the light of the characteristic termination of a chimp sentence. A great proportion of chimp sentences end with the chimp giving itself over to intense physical activity. Indeed, while the chimp is signing, one can see the potential energy build. The ape almost seethes until that energy is precipitated through a thunderstorm of activity. This same stress characterizes human concentration to some degree. I recognize this same process in my own behavior during periods of intense concentration. When I am working on a problem and concentrating most deeply, immediately upon the discovery of the solution I find I have to leave my office or otherwise dissipate a tremendous buildup of physical energy. The lesson of this is that the world of thought exists in tension with the world of the body.

All of this leads me to believe that there is a lot going on in the chimp's brain that it simply cannot get out because it has limited access to the propositional use of its own hands. The question is why? If those propositional talents are there, why can't the chimp use them? *I suspect that the answer is that nature is attempting to ensure against the kind of mistake it made with mankind.* And this brings us to the very heart of what philosophers call the mind/body problem, an octopus whose tentacles touch such concerns as the social scientist's with alienation, the psychiatrist's with schizophrenia, the classicist's with the Dionysian and Apollonian, and the critic's with energy and order.

What is clear in both the case of the chimp and also in human intellectual history, is that nature has given us more abilities than we are allowed to use. In the case of the chimp there seems to be an anatomical governor which keeps the animal's nascent propositional abilities firmly in a subordinate place when it comes to authority over behavior. In the case of mankind, we see that our ancestors, whose brains were anatomically identical to ours, had not nearly the access to their propositional abilities in organizing the conduct of their lives that we have. In their case, the constraints were not anatomical, but psychological through the work of religion. And so, what we can infer through the comparative example of ape and man is that as evolution elaborated our propositional skills, and in turn loosened some of the anatomical impediments to their use, it simultaneously established a series of cultural controls which attempted to curtail sharply the areas in which our propositional skills might be employed. The history of the West has been the gradual erosion of those cultural controls and the inexorable expansion of the role of our propositional modality in the organization of our lives.

The problem, from nature's point of view, is that to equip an animal to solve specific problems through simulation, it has to equip the animal with general problem-solving abilities. The danger is that the animal might start applying its problem-solving skills to other areas and disrupt a well-ordered pattern of adaptation produced through natural selection. Now, I am aware that underlying the foregoing is an unstated personification of nature, imputing to nature an interest in environmental harmony rather than chaos, and also imputing to nature the feeling that its authority is threatened by granting man and the other great apes license in shaping their behavior and their environment. The disposition of nature as a whole toward its various creations is well worth considering here, because to understand the cultural evolution of the West requires that one accept that "nature" is something more than indifferent to the product of selective forces.

There is an increasing acceptance of the idea that the environment is not simply composed of autonomously evolving entities changing solely as the result of fortuitous genetic variations. Instead, ethologists, biologists, sociobiologists, and geneticists are coming to believe that the environment and its constituents evolve together, in concert, and in communication in some way. Individual instances of this process are referred to as coevolution. Nature seems to perpetuate change along particular lines, and those lines seem to be influenced by the needs of the organism.

This is why one might argue that nature regards the development of propositional abilities as such a dangerous innovation. Produced fortuitously by the normal course of evolution, they bring with them the threat of chaos by giving the animal the means to rearrange both its own behavior and the shape of the environment around it. However, I do not mean to imply that the threat is in the mere act of usurpation; rather, the threat lies in the kind of program reason imposes upon behavior, and the kind of restructuring reason imposes upon the environment.

The fundamental difference between natural processes and abstract processes surfaces at the frontiers of theory, where the properties of abstraction itself begin to impinge upon and limit the understanding of the observed. This at least is my interpretation of Heisenberg's Uncertainty Principle. Simply stated, the Uncertainty Principle is that the electron, that fundamental atomic particle, cannot be isolated in time and space. As we approach certainty of its position we have to sacrifice certainty of its direction and speed; the better we predict its speed and direction, the less we can predict its position in space. The conundrum goes to the very basis of abstract thought. Analysis requires a point of reference on which to build a superstructure of rules. To be analyzed, a problem must be fixed along some axis; it needs to be abstracted or withdrawn from an undifferentiated mass of sense data. Thus, problem solving demands that at least one aspect of any problem be left out, and therefore any analysis is conditioned by the given of a problem—that aspect left out or taken as fixed. Analysis imposes bounds on the unbounded material it considers. It testifies to the rigor of science in that different sciences have become precise enough to discover these fundamental limits. But whatever the rigor of a science or the scope of a technology, it must, by the limitations of the information upon which it is based and the assumptions from which it proceeds, ultimately conflict with the analysis evident in the process of natural selection. We are equipped to make short-term adaptations to ephemeral environmental problems. There is an intrinsic, irresolvable tension between adaptations arrived at by our own egocentric analysis, and the analysis evident in the adaptive requirements of the ecosystem. And it is because nature has an interest in environmental harmony, evident in the interrelationships between the adaptations of individual species and the needs of the environment, that nature has attempted to constrain our simplistic meddlings in the ecosystem.

Sociobiology is a new, somewhat controversial branch of biology based upon the assumption that an organism some-times acts to its individual disadvantage if these actions enhance the prospects of survival of its "family." Sociobiologists claim that an animal does what's best to keep the gene pool healthy, rather than the individual. Some carry the idea further and theorize that organisms also perform tasks that do not benefit their survival, but serve some purpose in maintaining the health of the ecosystem as a whole. For instance, there is a bug which secretes a gas that helps to preserve the balance of the upper atmospheric shield. In fact, one can view the whole process of speciation as a means through which nature compartmentalizes her responses to maintain the balance of a changing environment. One can look at the environment rather than the individual as the adaptive unit.

Against the background of a holistic view of nature, the slow evolution of human intellect becomes intelligible. As I have noted, the recent past has seen no anatomical change in the human intellect, but rather a vast enhancement of its role in our lives. The brain was there in its present state all along (at least for the past five thousand years), but nature did not want us to use it the way we do now. If there is novelty in human evolution, it is that our most significant evolutionary battles have been fought on a psychological more than a physical level, and that at the heart of the battle has been nature's attempt to control what would appear to be an extraordinarily useful adaptation. In reviewing the evolutionary history of the human intellect, we see nature attempting to limit the power of an adaptation whose every application seems to enhance wildly the success of the creature that has access to it. The tension between the intellect and nature is the adaptive struggle turned inward. Produced in the normal course of evolution, propositional thought threatens the long-term prospects of the environment even as it enhances the short-term prospects of the individual. Consequently, while one set of evolutionary pressures works to expand the dimensions and role of the intellect, another set of pressures attempts to stem this advance.

If the pressures to limit the role of the intellect in behavior are the long-term needs of environmental harmony, the pressures that have militated for the enhancement of the role of reason in our lives are the equally pressing survival needs of our own frail species. As I noted earlier, there is a point at which dependence upon technological and propositional skills for survival tends to be self-perpetuating, because the choice to evolve in this direction lessens the crispness of what might be called a natural response. This point has been crossed by man, but apparently it has not been crossed by the other great apes. However, the crossing of this point led in turn to a series of usurpations as our novel propositional abilities spread through areas of behavior formerly reserved for responses prepared in the longer course of evolution. In turn, each usurpation has produced an ingenious counterresponse as nature has tried to maintain control over its unruly stepchild. As in the case of nature I am in effect personifying reason. I feel this personification is valid because reason is shaped by evolutionary pressures that derive as much from its utility to the community as to the individual. It is an adaptation that has a life of its own.

Devolving from this primal struggle are the central themes of Western literature and thought. In philosophy it is the mind / body problem; in intellectual history this struggle surfaces in the continuing vacillation between romantic and classical paradigms. However expressed, the tension between order and energy is the central preoccupation of the West. And if the first stage of the battle between reason and nature was fought on the anatomical level, the next stage we will consider is this contest played out on the reified level of the religious. The advent of consumer behavior, as we shall see, indicates the diminution of nature's authority on that level as well. Ultimately, the contest is one that reason can never win. The ultimate act of abstraction or displacement is suicide. As we also shall see, nature has now given us a final warning, a message of the futility and poverty of rational man. That warning is cancer, and it suggests that the end-game of the West may again be played out on the level of the anatomical. However, before coming to this grim connection, I will try to show in the coming chapter the signal events that have prepared the way for and indicate the purpose of consumer behavior.

~ 5 ~

Energy and Order

My hypothesis is that consumer behavior is not just a happy (or unhappy) accident, but is rather the product of a grim struggle that originated in the process of hominization itself. The struggle involves the competition for authority over our behavior between that awesome, momentous pulse of energy we personify as "nature" and a series of adaptations we commonly lump together as "reason." In the previous chapter I discussed the process through which man and certain other apes became anatomically equipped to usurp nature's normal role in revising behavior. With the lessening of anatomical constraints upon access to propositional abilities, the battle was joined upon the psychological level. This meant that having failed to maintain anatomical governors upon the use of reason, nature resorted to *religious* controls in an attempt to narrow the field in which reason might meddle. Because this chapter will cover an enormous span of history, its treatment of specific events will be compressed. Moreover, to show how various religious events fit within this evolutionary conflict requires that we take a new perspective on religious history.

Once again we might begin with a series of questions. Why did the ancient Jews replace a multiplicity of gods with one deity who was not of this earth? Why did the Greeks, while retaining polytheism, exile their gods to Mount Olympus, a place estranged from the field of the Athenians' daily endeavors? Why did Christianity dump the sins of the world on Christ and then replace the immediate vengeance of Jehovah with the notion of redemption through token penances? Why did

80

the Reformation remove the residual moral constraints on enterprise inherent in the holy path of Catholicism? The answer, which derives from the argument established in the preceding chapter, is that each of these events signaled the removal of a constraint upon the role of reason in our lives, and this same answer explains why modern Christianity and Judaism are utterly toothless as enforcers of good conduct in the earning of one's livelihood. The argument established in the last chapter also helps explain the contemporary resurgence of fundamentalism, pantheism, and other emotional forays into the sere heart of denatured religion, but before considering these current events, let us consider the previous series of events. Each heralded as an advance in religion, the effect of each has been to push first the gods and then God further out of our lives and to domesticate—in the case of the Reformation—what influence religion retains. That the retreat of religion from the life of the average European should be hailed as religious advance recalls the words of Willie Stark in Robert Penn Warren's *All the King's Men.* When asked what is morality, the Kingfish replies that morality is just two jumps behind what is necessary to do business, "But [society] is never going to stop doing business. Society is just going to cook up a new notion of what is right. Society is sure not ever going to commit suicide. At least not that way and of a purpose." We will consider now the forces that created the need to do business.

There are a number of myths that must be expunged before it is possible to objectively analyze a consumer society. The first is the myth of progress. We tend to think of a consumer society as the culmination of a march of progress that began when man first used a tool to hit an animal (or his neighbor) over the head. Actually, consumer behavior is the consummation of a way of looking at the world which only began to take theoretical shape about three thousand years ago. If there has been progress, it has been in the filling out and articulation of a cultural paradigm, but it is a mistake to interpret this paradigm as either the destiny or ideal of mankind. Anthropologist Marvin Harris argues that the ancient Egyptian enjoyed a better standard of living than we do today. If the goal of work is to create leisure we can see that the New Guinean, working a couple of hours a day, enjoys far more of it than we do. Indeed, Max Weber points out in *The Protestant Ethic and the Spirit of Capitalism* that one of the biggest impediments to the shift to capitalist economies was a tendency to cease work at the point at which laborers had secured a subsistence wage, rather than continue working after that point in the pursuit of profits. It is true that the West has reduced the physical effort involved in many endeavors. On the other hand, this has led to the degradation of the fitness of our citizens, who, in turn, wake up at the crack of dawn and run madly for miles as a kind of penance for this sort of progress. One of the most popular arguments for boosters of modernity has been the developments in health care. But this kind of progress might be looked at merely as an exchange of infant mortality for a host of adult afflictions. I look at progress another way: namely, that "progress" is the way reason sells its conquests to Western man. Instead of progress, the history of the West has seen a gradual *revision* of the way in which we view and act toward the world.

To analyze how and why, first let us take another look at the New Guinea Highlanders, this time as living representatives of the religious substrate out of which modern religions grew. Because they share with Europeans the materialism and avarice we associate with modern consumer societies, we might see in some of the Western cultural concepts they lack, ideas that developed in the course of Western history. For instance, Yali, a young New Guinean, had all the superficial trappings of assimilation into European ways, yet could look at the actual production of manufactured goods and still believe that the backroom activities of the ancestors who directed the operation were being hidden from him. Yali could look at the manufacturing process from start to finish and still not credit it to the hand of man. In a sense Yali was right. From his point of view there was something missing from what he was seeing, something the tricky Europeans were withholding. While the Europeans might have given Yali the secrets of cargo had they educated him from birth, they could no longer give them to him as an adult.

Where the European saw the work of intellect, initiative, and discipline, Yali saw the work of the ancestors. Yali was confident that his view was correct, because in his world, the ancestors mediated the products of the human intellect, disguising the origins of a technology in the process. In Yali's world the efforts of the individual counted for very little, neither did Yali credit the usefulness of secular knowledge. He had no concept of growth, of accrual, of progress, or even of time as cumulative and perpetual. Instead, Yali had the ancestors, embodiments of his tribe's unconscious, who mediated between the needs of the tribe and the needs of the environment. The ancestors in his view are nature's agents. They govern the tribe from the long-term perspective of the lessons of survival. To maintain their order they have to emasculate the role of the individual intellect. Conversely, for the intellect to have the behavioral latitude to intervene in the community's life, the ancestors must be pushed back; their influence must be displaced. This is what we Europeans have done.

The ancestors had to go because we had to survive. The maladaptiveness of ancient Semitic agriculture and husbandry is plainly evident in the transformations wrought by their practice over the centuries. What was a remarkably fertile crescent is now one of the more hostile environments on earth. The xerophication spread by overgrazing and warfare—the Assyrians salting the fields of the Clamites—and aggravated through overpopulation continues today, and now, five thousand years after this ecological malpractice first began, the perimeter of this man-abetted holocaust is one thousand miles deeper into Africa than it was in the time of Moses.

Both aboriginal human and animal populations tend to vary in proportion to the food supply. The radical foundation of Western civilization is that our intellectual forebears succeeded in making the food supply vary in proportion to human needs. Faced with our own maladaptiveness, we chose to adapt rather than die out. To do this we needed a world view that permitted freer adaptation and technological innovation. This in turn required that we revise fundamentally our relations with nature. And this required that we get the ancestors out of the trees and off our backs. As Toynbee and others have pointed out, one cannot exploit what one worships. Monotheism effectively decontrolled nature, clearing the way for the identification and exploitation of resources that had previously been protected by the sacred mantle of animism. In fact, the pattern of Western history has been to expand continually the frontiers of what may be considered a resource and hence exploited for profit. We will get back to this theme later.

The great shift that prepared the way for the development of Western technology was the cultural decision to desanctify and analyze the vicissitudes of nature, rather than to suffer them and worship their associated gods. This shift is the primary agon of Western culture; an original sin, an act of usurpation for which we still atone in our mythology and our dreams. But what was usurping what? I feel that our Greek and Semitic forebears were fortuitously selected proxies for the escalation of the evolutionary battle described in the previous chapter, a battle that began at the dawn of hominization. Monotheism marked the commencement of reason's *Anschluss* into the unconscious. Recall that consumer behavior is not just a question of wanting consumer goods; it is a question of producing them. There is no possibility that Yali might be a consumer without an elaborate restructuring of his view of the world. The advent of monotheism provided an ethical climate in which reason might prosper; it freed the hand of reason from the tyranny of the ancestors.

The prophets who proposed this new order were breathtakingly bold. In one imperial gesture, they laid out a revised view of human origins, an explanation for humanity's travails, and the foundations of a natural law which might permit mankind to exercise his capacities to manage and exploit nature to the fullest. This imperial gesture was the Book of Genesis. Should the modern equivalent of the Book of Genesis be proposed in the United States Senate, it would be dismissed as a partisan ploy serving the interests of the business lobby. Greatly compressed, the argument proposed by Genesis is this: First there is an all-powerful God, who created the universe. He happens to look like man, but, in fact, he created man to look like him. (How would the Senate react to the democratic announcement that it had been discovered that the universe was created by a Democrat, who created Democrats in his image?) Both the earth and man were summoned into existence to brighten His life. Because we were God's favorites, he gave us dominion over "the fish of the sea, and over the birds of the air, and over the cattle, and over all the earth, and over every creeping thing that creeps upon the earth." So far, so good. But then it becomes incumbent upon the Bible to explain why, if man is so favored, he finds himself in such a miserable estate. Genesis artfully uses this problem to deal with any lingering sense of animistic communality with the rest of nature, and then argues for the moral necessity of man's manipulation of his environment.

The Genesis myth has changed somewhat over the centuries, and one of the most intriguing aspects of early versions has disappeared in recent editions. In almost all versions, the contrast between man before the Fall and modern man is self-consciousness—the eating of the fruit of knowledge, which gives man awareness of good and evil. It is the contrast between innocence and experience. The element in the account of the Fall that has changed is the notion that before the Fall, man could speak with the animals. For instance, the Jewish historian of Roman times, Josephus, writes in his recounting of Genesis that ". . . all the living animals had one language at that time . . . [before the Fall]." This explicitly relates our alienation from nature to the advent of language. In later editions, this idea is broached only implicitly—the serpent *tells* Eve to eat the fruit—rather than explicitly. However, Genesis could not be more explicit in detailing the specific reason for man's expulsion from Paradise: it was our assumption of godlike autonomy by eating the forbidden fruit.

The metaphoric power of this usurpation of God's authority

is irresistible. Before the Fall the fruit was temptingly within our grasp, but proscribed. There is no better way to describe the unstable entente between reason and the natural forces that produced it. A gift from nature, it is also a threat to nature. The condition of mankind before the Fall described by Genesis is a very apt description of the role of reason in an animistic society.

As I noted when discussing cargo cults, the myth of the Fall shows up in animistic religions as well; however, as I also noted, the myth is somewhat underdeveloped in many animistic traditions. Its universality probably derives from an innate human need to account for consciousness and its attendant alienation of mankind from the innocence of the rest of nature. In the Judeo-Christian tradition the Fall is given an added role: it presents the ethical justification for man to undertake a more active role in the running of his affairs. Because man ate of the tree ". . . of which I commanded you, 'You shall not eat of it,' cursed is the ground because of you; in toil you shall eat of it all the days of your life." Knowledge, particularly man's usurpation of that knowledge, has turned nature from a patron into an adversary. Now, cast from Eden, man forever needs the cursed fruit of knowledge to survive.

Genesis, in all its versions, conveys the feeling that the Fall was inevitable, that what's done is done, and that man might as well make the best of a bad thing. To go back to our political analogy, Genesis is both a campaign platform, a legislative program, and a victory statement by our rational side. It kindly and insincerely offers a few conciliatory words for the loser— nature. Reason has now established its authority at the level of the unconscious, and the stage is set for the development of a world view that reflects the exigencies of reason.

I do not think that monotheism reflects the genius of Moses or the prophets, but rather was produced by the need for the human psyche to catch up with the human condition. I believe that the animistic bonds that keep reason subservient to nature began to break down as population pressures and maladaptive agriculture left the Semites in circumstances that became ever more austere. Reason replaced nature as the provider, and man needed an ethical system which promoted this reversal of evolutionary priorities.

Although monotheism was essential to the advent of Western civilization, it was not "officially" integrated with the philosophical and political tributaries of the West until Roman times. In the meantime, the philosophical, scientific, and political tributaries had their origins elsewhere in the Mediterranean.

THE PURSUIT OF CERTAINTY

It is interesting that the Athenians of classical times felt the same need to reduce the power of the gods in their lives which had earlier led to the advent of monotheism. In the case of the power of their gods, geographical situation and commercial ties and warfare brought the Athenians into contact with a variety of different technologies and world views. Nothing undermines the power of a parochial religious explanation of events so effectively as successful alternatives (heresies) to that religious explanation. The Athenians encountered a deluge of such anomalies. Faced with compelling evidence of Egyptian medicine and engineering, Hebrew law, Asian mysticism, Sumerian math, and so on, the gods took the prudent course and retreated to Mount Olympus rather than risk losing face in unsuccessful attempts to explain these novelties. Just as monotheism allowed the Hebrews to turn the intellect on nature, so this retreat cleared the Athenian mind for reason to offer up its account of the marvels of the universe.

It is possible to trace the gradual retreat of the Greek gods from the lives of Athenians through the study of Greek theater. And indeed, it is also possible to demonstrate from the same study that the ancient Greeks were aware of the hubris of reason, almost from the time reason was first unleashed. Greek philosophy and science contributed the outlines of a world view which it took more than two thousand years to fill out, and which we have not outgrown. Consumer behavior is in fact the apotheosis of the paradigm introduced by Plato and his confreres.

The ancient Greeks defined a universe that was lawful, bounded, and particulate. It was a universe of objects which act according to laws. The Greeks contributed the language of mathematics, which has enabled man to duplicate some of the feats of nature and partially to achieve Plato's dream of constructing a refuge for mankind safe from the vicissitudes of nature. But like the Hebrews, Plato and his confreres were proxies in reason's battle to broaden its beachhead in human behavior. In effect, the Greeks prepared man to be the tool by which reason might remodel nature according to its needs and properties. We have been well-paid proxies, to be sure, as no one can deny the cornucopia that has inured to Western man as a result of his embrace of reason, but the shift from animistic to rational world view turned us into strangers on our own planet. It has also saddled us with deep-seated psychic disorders: alienation, schizophrenia, and anomie. These and the other endemic problems of the West are the price of allowing a mind that is perfect, orderly, and immortal to attempt to rule a body and world which is evolving and transient.

With the advent of monotheism, this great shift was evident in the transformation of nature from man's patron into an adversary that must be tamed. This was also the case with the Platonic paradigm. In each case, the shift occurred at the level of perception. It might be best to use a modern analogy to show how two people may look at a common reality and see two different things. In the eastern theater of World War II, American soldiers reacted with great fear to the jungles of Melanesia. They were described as dark, fetid, and dangerous. On the other hand, the Japanese, to whom these jungles were only marginally more familiar, looked upon these same places as refuges. Japanese soldiers described the jungles as safe and hospitable, providing abundant food, water, and shelter. The difference lies in two different attitudes toward nature.

In *Apes, Men, and Language* I noted an experiment in which subjects were shown a deck of cards salted with anomalies such as a black queen of hearts. Jerome Bruner reported that the subjects would regularly report these anomalies as ordinary cards. Only with long exposure to such cards would the observers notice something amiss. Once the human brain has learned to fit sense data into perceptual categories, it will maintain those categories even in the face of pressing evidence to the contrary. This is the reason why the Melanesian cargo-cult leader might look at a factory and still believe that the products of that factory were the work of the ancestors. The ancient Greeks began the process of reorganizing our perceptual categories so that reason might usurp the role of the ancestors. What I want to do in the next few pages is to characterize some of the properties of this reorganization.

Through the good offices of Plato, Aristotle, Pythagoras, and others, reason established a set of new perceptual categories for the interpretation of sense information. To understand the nature of these new perceptual categories let us consider the suggestion I mentioned earlier, namely, that Western civilization was the result of a linguistic accident. Perhaps the best way to elucidate this suggestion is to contrast the way we perceive the world, as evident through our language, as opposed to the way the world was perceived by the traditional Chinese. China is a most intriguing example, because according to all tests of pure analytical reasoning ability, they are better equipped to be Westerners than we are. And yet the Chinese did not discover the abstract structures that constitute the Western world view, but instead exercised their abilities within the confines of a system of thought that lacked the enabling principles of science. Some sinologists, struck by the concreteness of Chinese poetry and art—Chinese art never discovered the principles of perspective which abstract the Western painter from his canvas—have come to believe that Western civilization is the product of linguistic accident. Outfitted with a Western education, a Chinese might design a nuclear reactor; while this same individual, given a traditional Chinese education, might see the world as a series of living analogies and harmonies which would prohibit him from understanding, much less designing, a nuclear reactor. Thus, traditional Chinese culture could invent gunpowder, the printing press, and the compass—inventions crucial to the development of Western technology—but Chinese culture could not contribute a set of principles that might generate a productive theory of explosives, or explain magnetic fields. As in the case of acupuncture, which is therapeutic rather than explanatory (the thrust of our medical research), Chinese culture would rather accomplish something than explain it. While Chinese technology and science functioned adequately in aid of the specific purpose for which it was designed, it lacked an abstract, logical language, such as math is for Western science, and which permitted the scientific efflorescence of the West. It is tempting, then, to accept the theory that Western civilization derived from a linguistic accident, because indeed, the only difference between Chinese raised with a Western education and Chinese raised with a traditional Chinese education is that the former has learned a new language. By this I do not simply mean that he has learned English or German, but rather he has learned a language that embodies a relationship to the world that is fundamentally different from the relationship evident in the language of traditional Chinese culture and science. This difference is worth pursuing a little further here because it focuses our attention on a dramatic event in the cultural evolution of the West, which is often passed over. That is the emergence in language of the verb "to be," an event which signaled the birth of an abstract consciousness in which reason might work unencumbered.

Ezra Pound and Ernest Fenollosa wrote a controversial essay entitled *The Chinese Written Character as a Medium for Poetry*. In it, they examine ancient Chinese ideograms, and contrast the properties of this system of writing with the writing and poetry of the West. They make the point that in the ancient ideogram, there was no such thing as an abstract state of being separate from harmonies and processes of nature. For instance, the ideogram for the evening sun depicted the sun *in the act of setting*. Rather than isolating such enduring Western concepts as redness or roundness, and then using these abstract concepts to *fix* the idea of the evening sun, the ideogram did not differentiate the sun from the situation in which it took on the properties we Westerners might abstract. Thus, claimed Pound and Fenollosa, the world of the ancient ideogram was a forthright, engaged, and processional world with no filter such as the copula which might mediate between the perceiver and his experience. This Pound and Fenollosa contrast with the world described by the Romance and Germanic languages of the West. The Western world is a world of states of being in which the locutor is separated from his experience by the verb to be. The verb to be assumes that there is a universal unchanging reality which is the setting for both perceiver and perceived. As opposed to the world manifest in the Chinese ideogram, this world is an enduring tableau composed of different agents, objects, and actions related by strictly defined law. The difference between the two is that the language of the West permits the description of a world having enduring qualities separate from the act of perception, while the world of the Chinese ideogram does not. For Pound and Fenollosa, this property of Romance and Germanic languages, which abstracted the locutor from the world, weakened poetic effect. It shifted the focus of communication from the undifferentiated appreciation and evocation of a particular event to the presentation of a denatured scheme of the event, organized by this abstract filter. It should be obvious by now that I am using Pound and Fenollosa to make the suggestion that in the West language evolved (they date the change in the West from the codification of Latin) in such a way that the perception and expression of experience was channeled through a rational grid. While this change might sap some vigor from poetic discourse, it permitted the West to take a posture toward nature in which technology and science might flourish. It is arresting, then, that despite contact with the West from classical Greek times, despite the manifest short-term utility of the Western way of looking at things, and despite culturally selected abilities that would enable the Chinese to quickly master Western ways, the Chinese have only assimilated Western culture and science in superficial and isolated ways.

All this would seem to give weight to the idea that the

development of Western civilization was the product of a linguistic accident, an accident that Chinese culture, with its strong, integrated, and successful relationship to the world, did not find useful.

The ancient Chinese ideogram has been described as "frozen-gesture": a holistic recreation of an "event." The differentiation between the object and the action it was involved in was minimal. The ideogram did not isolate the *quidditas,* the abstract properties of the object or action represented. Rather the actions and objects varied according to the scene. The ideograms portrayed a mutable relativistic world, a world profoundly different from the one described by the Greeks. Where the Chinese did not compartmentalize, the Greeks did. The ancient Chinese ideogram interfered little with the numinous mask of nature filtered through the unconscious. With the Platonic paradigm, increasing amounts of sense information were filtered through an abstract grid that sorted such information into discrete categories. It was a mechanistic world in which a scene was a composite or aggregate of different particles that operated in concert according to a set of principles. Its most profound point of contrast with the animistic world was the previously mentioned property of discreteness: the need to factor the world into bounded units.

Discreteness, as I argued earlier, is the limiting aspect of rational analysis. To operate, rational analysis requires a fixed point and a set of rules; a process of simplification that places reason in inevitable and eternal discord with nature. The Platonic paradigm attempts to solve reason's innate frustrations at attempting to describe a world which is mutable and open by supposing that the chaos of experience is a mask, underneath which lies an orderly, timeless universe. The Platonic paradigm thus boldly turns the tables on nature: the natural world is a mask; the real world is the bounded discrete world of the mind.

The importance of this shift in viewing the world cannot be overestimated. The way we view the world is illustrated by the way we act toward the world. Those original students initiated by a classical education had a predisposition to classify, analyze, and manipulate the world around them. It was not really a matter of choice, any more than Yali's belief in cargo was a matter of choice. Although as yet there is no literature on this question, I would not be surprised if, in the Western-educated brain, information is differently *routed* than it is in non-Western societies. For instance, an aspect of Western language often criticized in style manuals is the dead, neutered quality of words with latinate endings. While such words may not make for lively prose, they and their Greek antecedents serve the function of further separating symbols from their emotional charge.

Without going too deeply into semiotics, I might make the point that there is a fundamental difference between words that possess an emotional or religious charge and words that create an abstract category. Religious incantations, words of power, and other numinously charged words are integrated with affective powers, a relationship in which the symbolic properties of the mind are subordinated to the power of the unconscious. Greece contributed a language in which it was possible to free symbols from religious or emotional charge. It seems plausible that the process of freeing language and symbolic logic from the emotional freight imposed upon it by the unconscious must have entailed a neurological event: a rerouting of sense information.

The process by which language was abstracted from its emotional and religious baggage parallels the process I described earlier by which monotheism abstracted nature from the protective mantle of animism. The process might be called desanctification, but it really represents reason's assumption of control over the perceptual apparatus of Western man. The result of this desanctification was to replace animism with materialism. No matter how Christian ideologues might rail at the materialism and the lack of spirituality of modern society, they should realize that monotheism, and, as I shall show, Christianity, served the purpose of bringing these about.

The ancient Hebrews and the ancient Greeks prepared us to

look at nature as stuff, as material, as a resource suitable for exploitation. The Greeks assembled and developed the language and principles that were essential if we were to mold this stuff, while the Old Testament gave us religious sanction to do the molding. These two tributaries of Western thought finally merged during the Christian era in Rome. Actually, Rome is often cited as a protoconsumer society—godless, materialistic, wasteful, and consumption-oriented. But it was not a consumer society. It as yet lacked the relationship between the material appetites of its citizens and the industrial heart that is the genius of a consumer society. Rome exploited the wealth of its conquests, and not the material needs of its own citizens.

In Roman times, Christians were regarded as otherworldly religious fanatics. It is thus ironic that Christianity contributed two embellishments to monotheism that ultimately prepared the way for the methodical pursuit of worldly wealth. These embellishments and the final technological and political events that gave rise to a consumer society are the subject of the next chapter.

~ 6 ~

The Reformation
and the Gates of Enterprise

"Remember that time is money. He that can earn ten shillings a day by his labour, and goes abroad, or sits idle, one half of that day, though he spends but six pence during his diversion or idleness, ought not to reckon that the only expense; he has really spent, or rather thrown away, five shillings besides."
—*Benjamin Franklin*

The case I have been developing in the previous two chapters has been that certain events in man's physical evolution and in the evolution of the West reveal a gradual enhancement of the role of reason in its effect on human behavior and on man's interventions in the world around him. Monotheism and classical thought gave reason its work space in man's consciousness and the tools for the abstract definition and manipulation of the world. Now reason needed a work force to implement its reorganizations on a more mundane level than that of theory and theology. Reason needed, to use Weber's word, an ethos to encourage man's labors on a material plane. Reason needed to free its agent, the entrepreneurial spirit, from the constraints imposed upon it by communal and spiritual responsibilities, and it needed to encourage material appetites so that man might have inducements to effect these transformations. The Reformation paved the way for these final cultural adjustments that preceded consumer behavior. Although Hellenistic thought was midwife to the paradigm of rational man, a number of historical events had to take place before the paradigm might coalesce as the consumer society. Moreover, the "progress" from the first restructurings necessary to a technocratic society and their birth in the twentieth century was by no means in a straight line. From the golden age of Greece, through Roman times, Islam, the Reformation, the Renaissance, the Industrial Revolution, and through the advent of Marxist socialist states and consumer societies, every movement to increase the hold of reason on behavior has produced a counterreaction. The device that supplied continuity to these events, and allowed the incremental tightening of reason's hold on behavior was the advent of what Lewis Mumford calls man's extrasomatic intelligence—our ability to store, accumulate, and generate information in libraries and universities. No matter how barbaric the reaction to the cult of reason, a generation later thinkers might pick up where the past enlightenment left off. No matter that some piece of information is temporarily isolated by geography or politics from the mainstream of Western thought, once encoded there is always the promise that one day it will be joined with the other tributaries of Western thought. Without an extrasomatic intelligence to resist the most violent efforts to put reason back in its place, the human intellect would be incessantly refighting its first battles for a hold on behavior. The advent of extrasomatic intelligence gave reason a purchase in society at least partially disengaged from the cultural constraints that work to limit the intellect's power in a preliterate society.

If we look at Western history as the gradual freeing of the human intellect from cultural constraints that might act to limit the role of intellect, we see that Christianity offered an embellishment to monotheism that increased the moral scope of human enterprise. Then Christianity was modified itself to further improve the climate for man's industriousness. No matter that Christianity has messianic roots, or that the Reformation was a reaction to the perceived spiritual decadence of the Roman Church, or that the United States was founded upon pillars of religious and political freedom; each of these idealistic events abetted the quite worldly ambitions of the human intellect to extend its hold on behavior. Each of the events improved the climate for what the Church calls materialism.

We are not so much interested in the historical events that produced changes in monotheism as we are in the functional *effects* these changes had upon the relationship between man and his environment. The thrust of these changes—as we have said—was to desanctify nature, and through the notion of human autonomy to encourage man to manipulate his environment for his own purposes. But fostering entrepreneurial spirit, as the examination of cargo cults revealed, also requires vast restructurings of social relationships and their ethics as well. The individual has to see his interests as more important than his group's, and this requires the fracturing of communal bonds that impede the entrepreneurial spirit. Actually, in the underdeveloped world today, aid and development agencies regard the communal ties of tribal societies as a primary obstacle to development. Sharing in such societies is reinforced by both positive and negative forces: one wants to benefit from a neighbor's windfall, and one is afraid of retribution from both the gods and one's neighbors if one excels, or if one does not share some good fortune. Thus, ironically, we find do-gooders throughout Africa and elsewhere attempting to destroy a system where the wealth is shared by all, where orphans and aged are cared for, and to replace this system with the "screw-your-buddy" ethics of the West. Similarly, when missionaries first came to Tahiti, they were supremely frustrated because the Tahitians were models of Christian behavior, not out of fear of sin, but because that was the way one behaved, if one wanted to get by. This contrast is worth considering because it brings into focus one of the purposes of monotheism and Christianity: namely, to free the individual from social and ethical constraints that might impede enterprise and growth. The ethics of the encyclopedia salesman described in Chapter Two are not an aberration but the masterpiece of a long chain of events in cultural evolution.

From the missionary point of view, the absence of guilt concerning sex was proof that the Tahitians had fallen and of their desperate need to be saved.* On the other hand, without guilt or a sense of sin, the missionaries had no lever with which they might prise their way into the Tahitian conscience. Moreover, apart from sexual behavior, it was clear that Tahitian behavior was the very paradigm of Christian virtue. What troubled the missionaries was that the Tahitians behaved peaceably, not out of fear of sin and its consequences, but through natural inclination and social pressure. For the missionaries, virtue was not virtue unless it followed the conquering of evil. Anthropologist Robert Levy, who discusses this question in detail in *The Tahitians,* quotes the wife of a missionary who wrote about this "problem" in 1827: "I am far from considering the generality of [the Polynesians] true *Christians,* as many who make a profession [of their Christianity] want the essentials, which are, a sorrow for sin when committed, and a hatred of it afterwards."

The problem for this missionary's wife, as well as for many others, was that the Tahitians acted morally without any real concern for such abstract concepts as good and evil. To put it another way, the Tahitians had not yet tasted the apple, and not having fallen might not be redeemed. Robert Levy devotes a good deal of space to analysis of moral behavior in his little town in French Polynesia, and this section of his book contains the most incisive analysis in his study.

Levy uses the missionary wife's hesitancy to accept as virtuous the virtuous behavior of the Tahitians as illustrative of the problems a visitor coming from a "change-oriented" society has in understanding the behavior of individuals in a "steady-state" society. The missionary's wife comes from a society whose ethical system encourages growth and change, while the Tahitians's culture discourages change and encourages regularity. These differences demand entirely different relationships between the individual and his ethics. The

---

*Actually some of the best erotic literature to come out of Tahiti is found in the accounts of missionaries, who, though professedly shocked by the lust-crazed barbarism of the Tahitians, sent home exquisitely detailed descriptions of the sexual goings-on, and more often than not, embroidered the accounts with material from their own fevered imaginations.

European is equipped with a generalized set of principles which will serve him in novel situations. The necessity of change demands that the European assign relative priorities of goodness to different acts since change almost invariably involves transgressions. To quote Levy, "The moral emphasis now shifts from acts to intentions. For the consequences of the act cannot be judged solely by the ordinary and traditional goals and limits expressed in law and custom. The constant question now comes up whether an act is somehow good in terms of some other potential good. And it becomes important to know what it is that Abraham thinks he is doing [in sacrificing Isaac]." The European must be equipped to make ethical judgments, to be his own guide in uncharted situations.

While Western society encourages self-realization, independence, and change, the Tahitian "steady-state" sociocultural milieu regards these qualities as dangerous and attempts to encourage community harmony without equipping its citizens to play God. According to Levy, rather than using guilt to insure proper behavior, Tahitian behavioral controls involve such superficial devices as fear of embarrassment, ridicule, bodily harm, the law, and a host of other immediate forms of retribution. The Ten Commandments are interpreted, not as generalized laws, but as part of a series of specific things one should not do, if one does not want to run afoul of the community or the Almighty. "The emphasis," says Levy, "in contrast to missionary hopes is on external behavior, not intent."

Because, within the community, the things one does that are good or evil are well-determined and unlikely to change, it is not necessary for the good Tahitian to "integrate" his behavior at a level any deeper than a list of do's and don'ts. Levy notes that repenting to the Tahitians does not mean seeking forgiveness and God's grace, but, rather, mechanically performing ritual acts which will automatically restore one's proper relationship with the deity. There is no thought of an omnipresent, omnipotent force through which one understands one's relationship to the universe, nor is there any mysticism to the world view of the Melanesian or Polynesian.

The difference between the "steady-state" sociocultural substrate of Levy's little village in Polynesia, and our Western world view is also dramatic with regard to aspirations. Again to quote Levy:

> The value of a steady state is indicated in . . . a number of ways. The transformed Calvinistic God represents it. God, as I have noted, punishes people who become too proud, too ambitious, too innovative. He makes people sick who have too much property, who have come too far. He sends hurricanes into the world because westerners have tried to get to the moon. When things work out better than usual—in village affairs, in a family relationship, in fishing, or farming—whereas a striving western-er might be tempted to set a newer and higher goal, the villagers often consider it a matter of random good luck, a windfall, a kind of behavior, which suggests either "childishness" or else "fatal-ism" to missionary minds.

In contrast to the Tahitian, the European is not so much concerned with the immediate opprobrium of his neighbor as he is with his ultimate peace with his God. Thus he can ignore to some degree the needs of his neighbors in the pursuit of individual goals which, he tells himself, will ultimately inure to the benefit of all. His frame of reference for moral behavior has been transferred from his immediate environment to an unworldly set of principles. The function of such a system can be looked at several ways.

As Levy notes, the European, coming from a change-oriented society, needs an ethical system to guide him in uncharted situations since the *specifics* of misbehavior are regularly changing. The behavioral do's and don'ts of Polyne-sian society will not do. But why not, since, as the missionaries admitted, the behavioral do's and don'ts of the Tahitians amounted to virtuous Christian behavior? I suspect that there is another answer to the question besides the one Levy offers, although this answer is compatible with Levy's analysis. That is, that our European ethics are not merely a response to a change-oriented society, but an encouragement to change.

Tahitian ethics act as a kind of prior restraint, and they restrain not merely antisocial behavior, but are a force against change. On the other hand, the temporal distance between a Christian misdeed and retribution in the afterlife, and the ability through contrition to redeem transgressions through token acts, actually work to encourage transgression. By creating a space between an act and responsibility for the act, Christianity further freed the entrepreneurial hand. Moreover, since the price for transgression, whether it be a hundred Hail Marys, the purchase of an indulgence, or a charitable act like the contribution of a new wing to a hospital, was often substantially less than the gain realized by the act of transgression, there were further incentives to sin.

This is not to say that the Christian innovation of redemption occurred to create a society exclusively composed of robber barons. What the "culture" desired was an ethical system that promoted change not chaos. The Roman Church only slightly loosened religion's hold on behavior; enough so that some economic and intellectual ambitions might seep through the interstices created by the transfer of man's attention from his obligations to his immediate world to his "higher" obligation to a somewhat abstract set of principles. God was somewhat removed from the sphere of daily living. But not quite enough, as the Reformation ultimately demonstrated.

It is really the impact of the Reformation that reveals the functional purposes of its antecedents in Christianity. Having opened a door for the flowering of human enterprise, the Church found that the exigencies of commerce had frequently left the nascent bourgeoisie of the fourteenth and fifteenth centuries wondering whether their worldly success was going to cause them problems in the next life. Richard Tawney, in *Religion and the Rise of Capitalism,* reports that guildsmen, merchants, and even groups of money-lenders frequently sent emissaries to the Church for reassurance that their activities were not closing the door to heaven. Tawney notes that clerics began to complain of the "intolerable complexity of the problems of economic casuistry which pious merchants propounded in the confessional." And he follows by noting that "The Spanish dealers on the Antwerp Bourse, a class not morbidly prone to conscientious scruples, were sufficiently deferential to ecclesiastical authority to send their confessor to Paris in order to consult the theologians of the University as to the compatibility of speculative exchange business with the canon law."

While pangs of remorse might produce emoluments like the Cathedral of Notre Dame, the papal indulgence was clearly not a long-term answer to the stresses building between man's worldly ambitions and the strictures of the Church.

The Reformation was in part a response to these stresses, namely, to the corruption these stresses were causing in the Roman Church. Ironically, the Reformation abated this corruption by, in effect, sanctifying the sins. Luther, for instance, felt that religion should not be concerned with lists of do's and don'ts. He would rail against greed in general, but when asked for specific advice he would, in Tawney's words, "retreat into the clouds." With Luther in the clouds, godly men might scheme with abandon here on earth.

However, it was not enough to have the Church (up in the clouds) talking about salvation in abstractions. What was needed was a theology in which man's worldly ambitions were not just tolerated but encouraged. Those vestigial communal bonds that impeded commerce in the old Church, and which were retained by Luther in principle, had to be fractured if the entrepreneurial spirit were to flourish. There is no purpose in debating the point that this was not the intention of Luther and his fellow reformers. Indeed, as Weber, Tawney, and many others point out, Luther would have been appalled at the worldly way in which his message took shape. Still, as Weber wrote, "The effect of the Reformation (with regard to the religious conception of the calling) was only that, as compared with the Catholic attitude, the moral emphasis on and the religious sanction of, organized worldly labour in a calling was mightily increased."

It was up to Calvin to complete the work of the Reformation and articulate a modus vivendi that would allow the devout to do good and still do well.

Ironically, Calvinism and Puritanism did this by fixing the gaze of the devout entirely upon the other world, the world of eternal salvation. Puritanism was such an effective tool for worldly ambitions because, though it fixed the Puritan's attention on a spiritual world, the attainment of that world was completely stripped of all ritual and passion. "That great historic process in the development of religions," writes Weber, "the elimination of magic from the world which had begun with the old Hebrew prophets and in conjunction with Hellenistic scientific thought, had repudiated all magical means to salvation as superstition and sin, came here to its logical conclusion. The genuine Puritan even rejected all signs of religious ceremony at the grave and buried his nearest and dearest without song or ritual in order that no superstition, no trust in the effects of magical and sacramental forces on salvation, should creep in." Actually, when we integrate Weber's perceptions of the historical purposes of Protestantism with the grand pattern of cultural evolution we have been discussing, the ironies of this religious advance escalate to the point of cosmic laughter.

We have noted how monotheism and Hellenistic thought first pried man's attention from the communalities that bind him to nature. Christianity further freed the entrepreneurial spirit by creating a psychic window between act and responsibility. Protestantism seems to have performed a mopping-up operation, clearing nature's proxies—religious fervor and an emotional sense of sin—from areas where they might influence behavior. Calvinism displaced man's attention from the communalities that bind him to his fellowman, further loosening the restraints that inhibit worldly enterprise. Instead of direct attention to the sufferings of one's fellowman and the needs of the community, the Puritan best served his fellows by his absolute devotion to his worldly calling. This, in effect, permitted the devout to cheat their brethren and still feel pious about their ultimate vindication by a higher calling. These are the ethics of a "change-oriented" society that Levy contrasted with the earthbound do's and don'ts of a "steady-state" society. Weber describes the rationalization of this callousness succinctly:

It seems at first a mystery how the undoubted superiority of Calvinism in social organization can be connected with a tendency to tear the individual away from the close ties with which he is bound to this world. But, however strange it may seem, it follows from the peculiar form which the Christian brotherly love was forced to take under the pressure of the inner isolation of the individual through the Calvinistic faith . . . Brotherly love, since it may only be practised for the glory of God and not in the service of the flesh, is expressed in the first place in the fulfillment of the daily tasks given by the lex naturae; and in the process this fulfillment assumes a peculiarly objective and impersonal character, that of service in the interest of the rational organization of our social environment. For the wonderfully purposeful organization and arrangement of this cosmos is, according both to the revelation of the Bible and to natural intuition, evidently designed by God to serve the utility of the human race. This makes labour in the service of impersonal social usefulness appear to promote the glory of God and hence to be willed by Him.

Thus Christianity has changed from obedience to the imperative that if you hurt another you hurt yourself, to an imperative that ultimately translates to that if you help yourself you help others. This identity of self-interest and piety helps explain why so many entrepreneurs sprang from clergymen's families. In fact, if we look to the original model for the salesman or stump politician, we will find the evangelist. It is not surprising that children, noticing the way their all-too-fallen fathers manipulated their congregations, came to the conclusion that if it could be done for God, it might be done for profit.

The final contribution of the Reformation to the ultimate birth of consumer behavior was that it set the stage for the rational organization of human labor. From a means of providing subsistence, labor became a concrete form of devotion. Weber argues that prior to the Reformation, labor generally ceased with the securing of subsistence. It was not just that there were no incentives to work extra hours to accumulate surplus; it was, as I point out in *The Alms Race*, that many of the communal structures of traditional village life made it disadvantageous to accumulate more than one's neighbors. The Reformation shifted the villager's focus from his neighbors' to his own interests, and in sanctifying the sedulous pursuit of a worldly calling, created conditions that might encourage the flowering of the entrepreneurial spirit, and also supply a willing work force to implement entrepreneurial designs.

Weber, of course, directs his arguments to the advent of capitalism, and we are here discussing the advent of consumer behavior. However, the processes that Weber describes as essential to the development of the spirit of capitalism are part of the same, broad, evolutionary pattern that later led to the development of consumer behavior. Weber notes that capitalistlike behavior existed in ancient times in China and the Near East, but it was only with the development of an *ethos* that demythified the universe and permitted the rational organization of labor that a capitalist society might take shape. Earlier manifestations of capitalist behavior were *errata* that were prevented from fully flowering because religion and magic stood as obstacles to reason as a force in daily conduct. With the Reformation, reason had obtained sufficient hold on behavior that religion as an emotional force was expunged from daily life, and the content of religion itself was modified until religion served to justify the rational restructuring of daily life. This was the important news of the Reformation. With reason entrenched as a force in the economic, cultural, and religious life of the community, there could begin the articulation of scientific and economic theory without the meddlesome interference of the unconscious. The role of reason became formalized, and that a course of action was logical became sufficient justification for its undertaking. Society now had an ethos in accord with the need to do business. More importantly, society now had an ethos suited to achieve the "ambitions" of reason.

The Reformation indicated that the balance of power between reason and the unconscious had decisively shifted. The universe of the Calvinist was demythified and abstract, totally detached from the field of his daily endeavors. The world was now a blackboard on which reason might write clearly.

The Reformation directed man's gaze heavenward in order that he might be more effectively worldly. That is the crowning irony of this religious evolution. The heaven toward which he gazed was the same, crystalline, passionless world in which that pagan Plato sought refuge. Thought now reverberated entirely within its own estate.

One of the historical side effects of the Reformation—the colonizing of the American colonies—was the final tumbler in the series of prepared accidents that led to the advent of consumer societies. If we understand the process of Western thought to be the gradual freeing of the intellect from constraints that might limit man's flexibility and capacity for change, then there might be no more fortunate event than the religious oppression of the Puritan in England, an event that set the stage for the creation of a wholly change-oriented society.

~7~

Europe's Sin

The well-known words of Ben Franklin which introduced the previous chapter were part of a long, pitiless abjuration of all the temptations and impediments that stood between the worker and the total pursuit of profit. In this ethos we can see the roots of the need to sell. Such an ethos stands in stark contrast to the anti-materialist doctrines of the Roman Church, but also, upon examination, there appear to be marked contrasts that distinguish the practical Americans and their British counterparts. For a number of reasons the work ethic and entrepreneurial zealotry epitomized by Ben Franklin never developed in England even though there were substantial numbers of English referring to the same Calvinist or Quaker doctrines that unleashed American productivity. It is true that Britain has produced great entrepreneurs, but the entrepreneurial period in English history is described by economic historians as an aberration. There are too many environmental and traditional constraints to enterprise in Great Britain which devalue the rewards of the assiduous devotion to profit that Franklin and others promoted. Britain is a small island which, by the late eighteenth century, had developed virtually every arable acre of its land. Although for many there was now an ethos that might permit people to pursue opportunity, because there was no frontier, and because tradition was such a strong determinant of one's aspirations, the opportunities for those who remained in England were quite circumscribed. There were few rewards for those who devoted extra hours to their "calling," and

107

consequently, for the worker at all levels in Britain, one's occupation was primarily a means of supporting one's family and one's leisure activities rather than a path to redemption. In the colonies, particularly the American colonies, the situation could not have been more different, nor more patterned for the opportunistic ethos wrought by the Reformation.

Here was a continent of seemingly limitless dimensions, populated at first largely by peoples fleeing religious persecution at home and imbued with resentment over restrictions placed upon the human spirit in the name of tradition. It was a group not particularly inclined to limit its enterprise because such endeavors might conflict with a class consciousness enshrined three thousand miles away in England. If not wildly drunk on change, the Puritans and the Quakers were not subject to many of the conservative influences that obtained in England. I present this case cautiously and moderately, because as is well known, both Quaker and Puritan communities were in many respects quite conservative. However, what we are interested in here are the events that made these devout Christians such a fount of business acumen, entrepreneurial skill, inventiveness, and rationalism.

America has been described as Europe's sin. Its population is largely a legacy of various European sins against what have been termed the religious and political rights of man. The wages of these sins was the evolution of a rationally structured society which succeeded Europe in power and eroded European values; a society in which tradition had little voice in the face of the material blessings America promised. From the point of view of the gradual increase in the authority of reason over behavior which we have been following, America was the last frontier, because with the Reformation, the major remaining impediment to the rational reorganization of human society and endeavors was the force of tradition embodied in the political and social structures of European societies. Now Europe populated a continent far richer in resources than Europe itself with people skeptical of the divine right of Kings, a people who looked at most European arguments for autocratic social organization as a case of the emperor's new clothes. Different European kingdoms saw the short-term benefits of expatriating nettlesome religious minorities, as well as such potentially destructive elements as malcontents and adventurers. Had New England been colonized by people more from the mainstream of such societies, like the Spanish colonies in the American South and West, traditional ties of the old Church and society might have had a stronger bond on behavior, and America might not have become a fount of technological and social change. Indeed, even the difference between the innovativeness of New England and the English colony in Canada might partly be explained by the more English makeup of that colony. Instead, the colonizing of the American Northeast created a cultural time bomb with a population that had a genetic predisposition to restlessness and experimentation and an ingrained distrust of tradition.

The setting for this population was no less fortuitous. Resources are a function of technology and values, and for a time the richness of the continent eluded the imagination of those who hoped to profit from it. The vast forests were viewed more as a threat than an opportunity. The colonial attitude toward nature might be summed up by noting that forests were quite often termed "wasteland." This implied first that forests themselves had no value, and second that land not under cultivation was wasted. Unlike the aborigines they encountered on arrival, the colonists had no conception that nature had any purpose other than to provide food and materials for man. Moreover, the endless forests threatened the pilgrim's imagination with chaos and anarchy. When the Puritan searched for order he did not look around him, but into his own mind to the immutable, rationalistic doctrines of his church or to the strict Platonic order of his science. To the early American, nature was only beautiful when dominated or altered by man. These interventions were actually regarded as assisting nature, just as today forest managers make the argument that wilderness is better off when sensibly reorganized by man. In *From Know-How to Nowhere,* Elting Morison writes that some of the great early engineers, such as

John B. Jervis, felt that their works—the Erie Canal, for instance—showed a practical and aesthetic partnership between man and nature and benefited both. One cannot doubt the sincerity of this vision, but blind to the interconnections of the environment, it was also blind to the consequences of such interventions. It is generally believed, for instance, that it was through canals that the sea lamprey entered the Great Lakes—a dubious benefit to the fish that live there, and now, long after the canals have lost their luster, we continue to live with the ecocatastrophe they wrought. While the practical Americans might have been blind to the insults to nature of their projects, the Indians, because of their different balance between natural and rational authority, could see only these insults and not the logic that produced them.

While the religious origins of the Western ethos can be traced back to the dawn of monotheism, the philosophical roots are in Hellenistic thought. They took scientific expression in what is called the "cure-orientation" of science— namely, that science is a means of better understanding the forces of nature in order that we might then use these forces to cure human problems and improve the human condition. This conviction is endlessly restated by the engineers and scientists who established America's industrial and technological might in the nineteenth century. Morison points out that the engineers were doers for whom work was a calling; they had little life outside the world of their practical experiments and works. Later in the century, when these engineers were supplanted in importance by the theoretical minds who produced the second great surge in America's growth, this same notion of a calling obtained. And indeed, such callings, whether in the practical fields of engineering or in the more theoretical realms of science or in the arena of the marketplace, were never felt to jeopardize one's prospects for an eternal reward. There was no more godly pursuit than to investigate, devise, and then implement ways to tame and manage the forces of nature. The difference was that this calling was informed by reason, not faith, and that its ambitions were entirely worldly, and not directed toward an afterlife.

This mitosis of the notion of a calling inevitably began to create some tensions between the austerity of Americans' faith and the wealth and convenience that flowed from their worldly calling. There is a practical if not a philosophical contradiction in a faith that abhors ornamentation and comfort, but which applauds the devotion of one's life to the betterment of the human condition. At first, this contradiction was not so apparent as godly men devoted themselves to setting up the basic works of our society; however, with time, the betterment of the human condition imperceptibly began to blend into arguments for the increase of material comforts, the production of work-saving devices, and so on. Our godly engineers and industrialists, by the end of the nineteenth century, must have begun to have the same pangs of doubt as those that afflicted the bourgeoisie in pre-Reformation Europe. The problem was that work toward the betterment of mankind was informed by a vision that was broader than the religions that produced such a willing work force to implement it. This vision was the notion of progress. It transcended religious boundaries, and it, in turn, was informed by a notion of rational, autonomous, perfectible man. Let us consider briefly this ideal which not only justified the management and investigation of nature, but also the reworking of the political and social fabric of American life.

Progress assumed such tremendous importance in American life simply because there was no constituency for the more static models of the social universe. It was an idea that had been waiting to be born since the Renaissance, but which previous to its assumption of broad influence over American life had surfaced principally through the utopian writings and through implications of such thinkers as Locke, Descartes, and Hume. Morison writes that the vision described by the word progress "dominated the Western world for a century from the defeat of Napoleon at Waterloo to the pistol shot at Sarajevo in 1914." He goes on to say that the vision of progress had no one author and that "it fell somewhat short of exact definition." Two samples Morison provides are the phrases "one increasing purpose which through the ages ran," and, "the movement of mankind onward and upward forever."

They contributed a conception of human nature that viewed human dignity as founded in man's capacity for change and improvement through the exercise of his reason. Through the exercise of reason, man might manage his own affairs to improve the health of the community, as well as the rights of the individual; while by the exercise of reason man might also increase his control over the forces of nature and harness them to man's advantage. It is almost impossible to overstate the differences between a world view founded on the notion of progress and the steady-state world view that preceded it. As part of a Great Chain of Being, the peasant was presented with a fully explained world. While this seems confining, the peasant was liberated from the primary anxieties of the modern era—the search for an identity. With the collapse of the old hierarchies of society, the American had to forge his own identity. He had to answer questions that in other societies would be answered for him, and should he fail to rise as far as his compatriots, he had to justify his low position in society as he would not have to do in other societies. This was because this new world view was teleological in every respect. Not only was man the goal of nature, but a perfectly organized, strife-free society was the goal of man, and achievement within that society was the goal of the individual. Bound up with these notions of goals was, quite naturally, the notion of growth. The roots of capitalism were in the Middle Ages, but it was only with the gradual collapse of spiritual conceptions of self-worth that this concept might take on importance in the average man's conceptions of himself. We will have much more to say about these changing conceptions of identity a little later.

A number of notions that characterized or came to characterize "American" attitudes have now been presented: the notion of work as a calling, the notion that the management of nature might lead to the betterment of the human condition, the notion that society would be more equitably constructed, if it were rationally reorganized, and the notion that the history of civilization is marked by progress. Each of these notions had either a European root or counterpart. Indeed, the conditions for technological advance occurred much later in the United States than they did in Europe, and until the middle of the nineteenth century the United States—like Japan of the 1950s—was better at executing advances discovered elsewhere than doing the discovering.

Since the Renaissance, European life had been cyclically seized by classicism and rationalism, and yet these periods did not have enduring, transformational effects on society as a *whole*. European society, developed and mature, retained too many legacies of the past to offer its average citizens the opportunities, the mobility, or even the expectations that were presented to the American. Rejecting the injustices of the past (something that was a delicate issue in Europe), Americans looked to the future, and by a process of elimination arrived at reason and common sense as their guide. The material and social rewards that derived from this posture were more than enough to nourish an optimism (which if one believes in progress is the only consistent mental attitude one can assume) that soon came to be our national characteristic.

There was most decidedly "progress" during the period Morison describes as the era of progress, the most widely cited example being the decline of infant mortality. There can be no doubt that this period was marked by real advances in the standard of living. However, an index like the standard of living is measured, as economists like Samuelson have belatedly noticed, solely in material terms, and somewhat crude material terms at that. Contained therein is the assumption that the quality of life is judged solely in terms of material rewards. Moreover, as has been pointed out endlessly, such measures of progress omit consideration of the "price" for that very progress: The deterioration of health, the degradation of the environment, and the increased incidence of such diseases as cancer, ulcers, and the like. But I am not so much interested in taking a revisionist view of the standard of living as I am in examining why it had such a mesmerizing hold on American consciousness for so long. Clearly there were costs to the increase in the standard of living. Not just nonmaterial, but material costs as well, such as the increase in stress-related diseases, or the decline of craftsmanship as mass production expanded through industry. Yet, in American consciousness, the trade-offs for increases in the standard of living were, until recently, given very little weight as compared with the benefits that followed from economic growth. This implies that there was something more than objective judgment behind our belief in progress. Rather, progress was a myth: it held a numinous thrall on the imagination. Moreover, it was a myth that took on the proportions of a religion since it offered an explanation of the human condition, and it served as a guiding principle for the organization of one's life. Eventually it came to supersede in importance the more austere myths that gave Americans the ethos presumably capable of improving the standard of living. The Protestant ethic produced a work force willing to suspend gratification, willing to subordinate its lives to the dictates of a "calling." Progress rather than heaven came to be the justification for this self-denial. The palpable, material rewards of the work ethic ultimately placed a more compelling claim on the imagination than did the dour proscriptions of the faith. It was not just missionaries who intended to do good and ended up doing very well.

Behind these apparently simple transformations in the American world view there lurked the competition between man's intellect and nature. Progress was reason's myth, and the promise of material rewards was its litany. What we perceived as progress were the gradual transformations of the world and our lives that occurred in adapting the world to our new way of looking at things. Progress was the filling out of a new gestalt. In working for progress, we were (and are) reason's pawns working to create a more rational world and society. We did not and do not control reason, but rather reason controlled us. Reason is a natural force that during the course of human evolution took on a life and evolutionary history of its own. Like Yeats's rough beast, it was waiting to be born.

At the dawn of the Industrial Revolution, there was the perception that something novel had been loosed on the world.

William Blake described reason in Satanic terms, an intuition that resonates today. The evidence of both the charismatic Christians and the desiccated formal religions of today is that there can be no marriage of the intellect and faith. Here again we encounter a conundrum because a central theme of this chapter has been that reason became a faith. This brings us to the core of genius of a consumer society. I use the word genius because consumer behavior breaches a fundamental impediment to reason's total control of behavior. Recall that while a paradigm of reason is a myth, there is a fundamental difference between the rational cosmos and religious cosmos. In the rational paradigm, the pattern-making properties of the mind are influenced by information that in all probability takes a different routing through the brain. The long process of usurpation gradually exiled those aspects of religious behavior that could not be rationally managed to areas of behavior peripheral to the conduct of one's life. It was what happened at this point that led to the emergence of the consumer society. It is to these events and the structure of society that emerged from them that we now turn.

~ *PART III* ~

Managing Man and Nature: Apotheosis of the Intellect

Part III presents the idea that consumer behavior is an artifice which evolved to enhance the power of reason as a force managing man and nature.

~ 8 ~

Capitalizing on Discontents

The pattern of decision-making that I feel characterizes a consumer society did not take a broad hold of American life until after World War II. Thus, when we talk about America as a consumer society, we are speaking about the last thirty or so years. Today, there are numerous indications that the era of the consumer is ending in its heartland, even as consumer values are spreading into virgin territories throughout the world. The events that ultimately produced consumer behavior trace back to the dawn of human history, and in that scale, the life of consumer behavior is but the briefest flash. The consumer society really is a cultural epiphany, the brief realization of a scenario forecast at the dawn of Western thought. The slow cultural movement toward a rationally managed society, which we have been describing, culminated in an artifice that permitted reason to harness the very religious content it originally exiled, in order to expand its hegemony in behavior and the environment. To set the stage for a consideration of the nature of this artifice, consider Euripides' play the *Bacchae* and examine a problem posed 2,300 years ago which the consumer society has "solved."

The problem was posed in this parable of the dangers of a skeptical and rationalistic society. Pentheus, the skeptical king, refuses to acknowledge the power of the new cult of Bacchus that is sweeping through his kingdom. Pentheus scorns the new god and the self-abandonment he commands as devotion.

On the other hand, wise old Tiresias, a survivor of many

119

wars and upheavals, recognizes that Dionysus is not a god to be denied and, although he is ridiculed by Pentheus for looking ridiculous, he joins the dancing in the woods. Pentheus prides himself on his clear-sightedness and objectivity, but Dionysus, denied by Pentheus, subverts Pentheus's perceptions with phantasms and hallucinations. Pentheus blindly walks into the middle of the celebration, where he has his head torn off by his own subjects.

The play, like most classical tragedies, is a warning to those who risk the hubris of denying a god. But the particular form of retribution makes the play a dramatic personification of the dangers attendant to the human psyche contained within the then-emergent model of rational man. Pentheus, the embodiment of rational autonomy, denies the power of the god, who demands abandonment of self-control and whose power is expressed through orgiastic celebration. Pentheus's objectivity cannot permit him to abandon himself; in so doing he would be subordinating his intellect to the natural forces embodied by Dionysus. For Pentheus, autonomy means self-control; control over his kingdom in the macrocosmic terms of the play. The play spotlights the absurdity of this posture. First, Pentheus gradually loses control of his formerly well-ordered kingdom as his subjects are swept up in the Dionysian fever. Then Euripides shows the fundamental absurdity of rational autonomy by having Dionysus pervert the very perceptual matter upon which reason works. The point could not be more clear: reason is dependent on nature for its very life, and upon the senses in particular for the raw material of its machinations. To believe that reason might control its very source is to dangerously neglect natural forces. Euripides' description of what happens once these forces are denied is even more intriguing. They turn subversive. Ultimately, they bring reason into fatal conflict with its own subject matter. Pentheus's purposeful ignorance of the authority of nature alienates his mind from his body in the most vivid possible way—he has his head torn off.

The *Bacchae* provides a model for the consequences of denying the authority of the gods that is reflected in Jung's descriptions of the psychological pathologies that occur when one denies the contents of the unconscious. More to the point, the *Bacchae* might have been a metaphor (as several astute theater companies realized) for the state of the Union in the late 1960s. A rationalistic society, alienated from nature and religion, was besieged by its young swept up in a Dionysian fever. That "threat" was more theatrical than real, but it was no coincidence that it took the form it did. What is arresting about that upheaval as well as the "irrational" upheavals that preceded it, and the smaller fundamentalist religious movements that have followed it, is that the way these "revolutionary" movements have been domesticated indicates that in the 2,300 years since Euripides wrote the *Bacchae,* reason has come up with an answer to the problem Euripides threw at those who believe in rational autonomy. That answer is consumer behavior. Euripides, acting on sound intuitions, presents the case that the rational world view makes an enemy of nature, which will ultimately subvert and topple reason's edifice. The consumer society presents reason's answer, which is that these exiled and potentially dangerous forces can be used as a power source which rather than undermining it, further enhances reason's authority. Before considering the long-term implications of this gambit in reason's chess game with nature, let us look into the workings of this ingenious cultural device.

In the previous chapter we described the circumstances that gradually moved reason to a central place in the organization of our society and our lives, exiling in the process the irrational forces of tradition and religion from their accustomed role. If we can attribute an ambition to reason once it had established its place in society, it would be to reorganize life in a predictable, manageable way. Its promise for man was to free him from the vicissitudes of nature and take the element of chance out of his daily life. It promised Plato's dream of a refuge from ceaseless change. And so man, pursuing a rational, technologically managed society, was pursuing certainty: the certainty that a child when born would survive, the certainty that man would not constantly be

suffering the blind curve-balls of nature; release from the
uncertainty of food supply and disease; and release from the
onerous burden of catching game, scraping fields, fleeing wild
animals or natural disasters. The price in this Faustian
bargain was a sense of place in nature. In order to create our
managed universe we had to suffer alienation from those parts
of ourselves that connected us viscerally to the natural cycle.
The price of material certainty was a metaphysical uncertainty
of who we were. Our worldly success left us trapped between
the sky and the earth.

This alienation was not merely a psychological problem.
Just as the rational world view exists in tension with the
irrational content it denies, so does a managed ecology exist in
tension with nature. Great energy is required to maintain
each. The construction of a psychic and material island of
order created psychic and material disorder, and also set in
motion forces seeking to resolve the imbalances these psychic
and material oversimplifications entail. It turns out that this
very imbalance provides the fuel and momentum of a consumer society.

In the introductory chapter, I presented the idea that there
is a consumer decision at the point of which the consumer's
better judgment is recurrently overruled by powerful emotions
and anxieties. Our consumer is somewhat like Pentheus,
subverted by a part of himself he does not recognize and
hence cannot control. Each decision is like a little madness.
We are now in a better position to understand the "work"
these decisions perform. That there is an organization to the
momentary madness of sales becomes clear when we examine
the mass equivalent of the consumer decision. We discover
that the structure of the consumer decision, as it occurs in
such individual phenomena as encyclopedia sales, also applies
to mass behavior such as fads, fashions, and even broad
cultural movements. In the sale, the fad, or the cultural
movement an object or an activity is invested with an
emotional importance that supersedes common sense. However, it is not just that there is a similar structure to these
decisions at the individual and cultural level, it is that there is

a purpose that integrates these individual madnesses into a coherent system. The set of circumstances in which anxieties are harnessed for profit is replicated throughout a consumer society, and this process is its foundation. The novelty of a consumer society lies in the way the profit motive itself is harnessed to provide the "work" in increasing the rational management of man and nature. It is at this level that the coherence of a consumer society begins to become apparent. An interesting way to introduce this point might be to consider the history of one of the most dramatic expressions of discontent of recent years—the counterculture and its cultural center, the rock-music scene.

STRIP-MINING THE IMAGINATION

Rock music is in what some performers optimistically term a backwater. It has been for years. This does not mean that there has been a radical abatement in the number of new musicians offering their songs. Rather, rock's receding energy is apparent in the diminishing import of the musicians themselves. No new sound has the momentousness of that of Dylan or the Beatles, nor do Dylan and the Beatles any longer seem momentous. Concerts do not have the mobilizing effect they had in the late 1960s. New musicians of genuine talent burn out at the very point at which they should be starting to develop, and radio stations are playing so many hits of past decades and new versions of old songs that a person awakened from a long sleep by a clock radio might be confused as to what year it is.

For one week in the fall of 1969, much of the nation was seized with a rumor that the Beatle album *Abbey Road* contained a coded message of Paul McCartney's death. The rumor started as the result of a graduate student's twisted hermeneutical reading of the album design and some lyrics played backward. What it showed was that the Beatles' charisma existed in our imagination; the Beatles were not fascinating, we blessed them as fascinating. A Beatles' concert was a collective epiphany because the audience willed it so. The rock stars of the sixties have not lost what made them momentous; rather, the audience no longer gives them moment. Some would argue that too much history has come between the musicians and their audience, but something seems to have come between virtually every group and its audience—if the two still meet at all. What is missing now is the transformational energy that invested the world of rock for a brief moment in the last decade and in whose glow the rock scene peaked. It was a property of rock that its truly liberating moment passed so quickly that it aroused nostalgia almost as it occurred. Dig up some old records and listen to them now. It should become clear that as much as it was music that made the rock scene important, some life force lent importance to the music.

Intense collective movements, such as the rock scene, are an increasingly recurrent phenomenon of American life. They are visible every day in the little tremors called fads, and even more prosaically in the constantly shifting assignments of value which different groups within society unconsciously confer on people and objects. These assignments of value can seem absurd to people outside the cultural niche where they are made. An artist told me of an exhibit where a woman offered to buy a simple work fashioned out of string. The price was high, about $1,000. The artist accepted the woman's check, then crumbled the string work into a ball, and handed the buyer her new acquisition.

What is at work transforming a ball of crumbled string into an object of value also operated in the massive transformation by which rock took on the illusion of being a world movement. A run on a particular style of art, a fad, or a gigantic cultural spasm such as rock all reveal the temporary focusing of some energy loose in America. The fad fulfills by expressing some previously pent-up energy. However, this energy has its own laws, and the artist or pop star who taps potent forces in his audience also constructs a prison of his audience's expectations. His power will vanish should he abuse the illusions he has unknowingly encouraged the audience to develop. The booing Dylan received when he first used amplification and a rock back-up band was a mild example of this. Now Dylan is into disco, once more betraying the expectations of his aging audience.

Audience, however, is not the proper word for the original constituency of the rock scene. It was rather a medium through which outlaw energy could be expressed, just as rock music was the palpable expression this energy chose. Rock was outlaw music and its celebrants reveled in violation of the norm. Now rock has faded in the embrace of the Establishment that originally called it outlaw. And it appears that the rock scene never really posed a threat to American society or promised a new culture. Even before it expressed itself politically, it had been subtly harnessed for an inimitably American purpose.

Although it was originally perceived as outlaw, the rock scene was a collective expression of the mode of behavior I have been describing for the encyclopedia sale. Politicians, salesmen, and the advertising world have long known that even the most commonplace decisions can be more effectively influenced by tapping irrational wishes or fears than by appealing to reason. And it is not just the mainstream of America that can be influenced. The temporary ascendance of unreason over reason in times of decision is a particular behavioral configuration. The history of the rock-music scene shows that the behavioral configuration surfaces not just in individual behavior, but also in mass behavior and even characterizes the actions of those who would consider themselves fundamental enemies of the consumer society. The irrational, frustrated by an increasingly rational world, turns outlaw; however, it is only perceived as outlaw in its larger and more intense eruptions, and even there, wherever a pool of this outlaw energy collects (identified by business as "consumer interest"), it is immediately capped by a corporate superstructure whose sole purpose is to tap it for profit.

The rock scene was no exception, and its earlier vitality easily supported an enormous industry. But the dissatisfactions, repressed needs, and anxieties in the young that supplied the rock scene's life energy are also basic to the consumer personality. The record industry skillfully brought out of latency the consumer aspects of the rock scene. The rock that at first offered a promise of liberation soon became a need—something to be consumed. Now no sooner does a musician who inspires "consumer interest" emerge than he is strip-mined for "product" to feed to a rootless mass of rock consumers. The average life span of a new rock presence is at present a little over a year, and it's getting shorter all the time.

Hollywood is the center of the rock scene now, and if the consumer personality is the kernel of the American way of life, Hollywood expresses its fullest flowering. Its importance to understanding the rock scene's detumescence is both symbolic and factual, but in Hollywood where symbol ends and fact begins is unclear.

In myth, Hollywood is where the symbolic wash of American imaginative life is turned into corporate fact. Everywhere Hollywood's pneumatic facade reflects this effort to remake in material form images stripped from the imagination. However, the dreams mapped on Hollywood's topography are without mystery, and this also is in accord with myth, because Hollywood is the refuge for people and arts that are cut off from their roots. Arts, once dead, migrate to Hollywood to live on parodies of their former life. This zombiedom has long been Hollywood's double-edged joke on the nation.

The profane pilgrimage to Hollywood grew out of the rock scene's consumer susceptibility, which undercut the music scene from the beginning and which exposed its central myth—the myth of solidarity, the myth that to the counterculture, rock was "our music" and the musicians "our people." It is a fiction assiduously courted because it is essential to the theater of rock. But it was splintered, in part by the musicians' vigorous pursuit of the fruits of rock's consumer attributes.

The radical musician spent his day with agents, record company executives, publicity people, beautiful people, and various commercial sharks. While he is with these executives he or his representative are bargaining like thieves to make sure every possible dime is extracted from "his people." Bill

Graham, the rock impresario, complained that it was the rock musician's cold-blooded demand for ever higher ticket prices and ever larger theaters that led to the closing of the Fillmores and is leading to the end of the rock concert. The only artist he knew who insisted that ticket prices be kept low was Joan Baez.

Phil Ochs came to the place he considered the end of the world because he felt that the life force had disappeared from the rock scene, and as he put it, "when you don't feel the life force the next best thing is to be fascinated with its opposite." Ochs, a cherished figure of the radical left, had all but ceased writing songs, and may himself have come to the end of the road in Hollywood. Ochs felt that the "organic" period of rock was the years from Dylan's "Like a Rolling Stone" through the era of the Beatles. He felt that despite heavy commercialization this period retained enough vitality to remain healthy. "Then came psychedelic music," said Ochs, "which I never liked, and which in retrospect I think was incredibly damaging to the country and to music." Ochs expected that music would merely continue to get more commercial and "less musical." Phil Ochs killed himself.

Rock or any popular art in America is going to be commercial, but folk and some forms of rock are nourished by roots in experience and in relationship with the audience. The musician in Hollywood comes into contact with all the concentrated commercial pressure America has to offer. His record company will demand "product," he will be promoted in the crassest way, and often he will be an object of contempt to the very people strip-mining him. The pressures can break even those musicians who are frankly commercial. Chuck Negron of "Three Dog Night" found himself run ragged by the appetites of his record company and his audience. On one occasion his group presented an album cover they had designed to the president of their record company. The president looked at the cover, threw it back at them, and screamed that they were going to shoot a new album cover and that this time "I want balls! I don't want faces and new haircuts."

To his record company, Negron was the "product," but he was also dehumanized by his audience, an audience that has now completed its evolution from medium for outlaw energy to mass-consumer mechanism. It is here, in the breakdown of the rock concert, that the myth of solidarity collapses for good, and it becomes plain that rock is not in a backwater, but a fast-drying gulch. In the waning years of the rock scene, the hysteria of the audiences attained a life of its own, and came to compete with the performances. Performers who used to encourage bacchic excess came to feel discomfited by the devouring appetites of the younger audiences which reduce the performer to a mere device by which the crowd can "get off."

Hysteria has always been a property of rock, and the argument could be advanced that its persistence is a sign of health. But the cathartic aspects of the concert used to be the culmination of a definite development. The communion between the musician and the audience was the marrow of the rock-music scene, and the wonderful variety of concerts and musical occasions was the tissue of rock's life-style.

Although press agents still invoke some hushed rapport a new star has established with his audience, in fact, there are few places left where that hushed rapport can occur, and managers are increasingly relying on "packaging" to get new musicians known. Packaging can get a musician from obscurity to the grandest arena without any apprenticeship at all. It means that in order to book a manager's star group, the theater also has to take an unknown group the manager is currently pushing. This, said Graham, is another practice that makes it difficult to present a well-organized concert. The disappearance of places to perform also stifles the more creative and exploratory musicians who are essential to the health of any music scene. The few arenas left naturally prefer proven boffo draws, and although the record companies still release hundreds of albums every month, most of these are stillborn, because virtually all promotional money is channeled back into the stars who are making money in the first place. At every point in its evolution the rock scene has become more intensely and nakedly commercial.

I used to enjoy rock. Now when I think about and get depressed by its current estate, I remember something song-writer Randy Newman said to me earlier. "The one thing I take comfort in," he said, "is that they don't know what makes a hit. If they did, they would manufacture them, but they just don't know." There is more hope in these words than could be dampened by a dozen Sex Pistols. Once a group hits, the industry might plunder it, the audience, and the music, but they are impotent without some intimate chemistry between the performer and his audience. No matter that the rock scene is reduced to the lowest commercial terms, it is redeemable because no corporate attempts at cloning can duplicate the work of the imagination.

Yet perhaps the best thing is that although the rock scene has died, its end will in no way resolve the conflicts that were the source of its power. That bacchic energy, still outlaw in America, will build, and when it erupts again musically it will come with that same exhilarating intensity that marked the beginning of the jazz age, the swing era, and the rock age. At least for a moment it will be free of the heavy weight of executives, of critics, and of the consumer society which, just as it spawned it, will devour it.

So long as every outbreak of this energy is followed by a sales boom, we can be certain that the consumer society is in perfect functioning order. What should be clear is that the coherence of the consumer society is on the level of the structure of the consumer personality: which activities or products become invested with emotional urgency that is ultimately expressed in a material appetite is the result of chance. Once it appears this appetite galvanizes corporate America to standardize, manage, and deliver whatever it is that satisfies the appetite that has surfaced. And this residual-ly expands the ambit of reason into ever-new areas as the corporate superstructure seeks to ensure the availability of whatever it is the consumer wants to buy. This process is readily apparent as the concept of farming expands to include specialized areas. We now have tree farms, eel farms, fish farms, and worm farms. Recently, French agronomists an-nounced that they had discovered a way to farm truffles, a delicacy which had nobly resisted the blandishments of the managed life. Nature has not merely had its authority displaced from human behavior; with each year it finds more of its domain managed or brought to extinction by man. Ultimately, as the parable of Pentheus tells us, being managed or brought to extinction amounts to the same thing. It is fundamentally irrational to believe that reason can manage nature. Apart from the biological truths that reason depends for its life on nature and not vice versa, we can see from the nature of the consumer mechanism that the demands for growth that are innate in a consumer society inevitably lead to the surpassing of the sustainable yield of the "resource" being tapped. Boom and bust is the rhythm of a consumer society. The cycle that I applied to the rock-music scene, also applies to the management of natural resources. The pressures for management of some particular animal or plant are the pressures for increased yields. This increase has to come from somewhere, and if it does not come from the resource's future, it comes from some perturbation of the resource's environment or genetic structure that sets in motion counterreactive forces.

The thing that permits us to ignore the rather alarming messages to this effect, which are surfacing with increasing regularity, is the flexibility of the consumer mind. With our unconscious ties to the natural order of things all but severed, we have no commitment to any particular organization of nature or even to the survival of any creature other than ourselves. When we exhaust one particular vein of consumer interest and the resources that support it, we blithely move on to a new area. Consumer optimism, founded on the belief in technological progress and discovery, always promises rewards that serve to obscure our perceptions of what we have wasted or lost. The consumer society and the consumer personality are not really committed to any particular form of society; they are rather devices to aid the rational management of whatever uncontrolled phenomenon they encounter or, as the case of the counterculture reveals, produce. This is one of the great ironies of a consumer society: each problem the rational management of society or the environment produces further enhances the sweep of reason. Like the doctors during the Black Death, in attempting to cure the symptoms we actually spread the disease.

What is the disease? I have been writing about the most irrational aspects of modern life—sales crazes, fads, outlaw cultural movements—in terms which argue that they advance the cause of reason. Clearly, the rock-music scene does not fit into our ordinary conception of a rational society. However, as I have stressed, the effect of the consumer evolution of the rock-music scene was to bring under management a part of our cultural life which by any account would seem to be the most profoundly Dionysian and uncontrollable urge. The disease then is subordination of a phenomenon to whatever rational program will increase predictability of the future of that phenomenon. It is the pursuit of certainty; the pursuit of an orderly predictable world safe from the vicissitudes of change—the world Plato had envisioned in the *Phaedrus*.

I refer metaphorically to this process as a disease, and I used the image of the Black Death. But the disease that has most often been used as a metaphor for modern society is cancer. Indeed, it is almost irresistible to speculate on the parallels between the structure of a consumer society and the disease its every activity seems to produce. The relationship of the consumer personality to both its host and the world is similar to the way cancer is described as relating to its host. Like the consumer personality, cancer imposes its own organization and simplifications on the resources of the body. Cancer is a lethal simplification of cellular functions which ultimately overtaxes the reconstitutive powers of the host. Cancer usurps the body's authority over the cells and strips them of every function save growth. In short, cancer farms the body the way we farm the earth. It perturbs natural processes in order to exaggerate and control some isolated characteristic of a given phenomenon.

I have argued that simplification was in the nature of reason. That phenomenon had to be fixed on some particular axis in order to be analyzed, and this set reason into fundamental discord with nature. The metaphorical marriage between this characteristic of reason and the relationship of the cancer to its host is so compelling that we must wonder whether cancer is, in fact, the biological correlative of reason. What is so mystifying about cancer is that it has no common substance other than the fact that in each of its various manifestations the cancer applies its own set of laws to the material it is dealing with. This also is what is so intriguing about consumer behavior: it is a set of laws that affects the way a person perceives and relates to the world. This is why one cannot escape the consumer society by simply removing oneself to the South Seas, and this of course presents a basic difference between metaphor and reality. One can remove oneself from many of the causes of cancer.

I will not attempt to detail the exact neurology of the consumer personality, for that is beyond the ambitions of this book. However, I do feel that something novel in the consumer mind is influencing the sequence of the consumer's perceptions. We saw in the examination of the encyclopedia sale alterations of the buyer's state of mind that verged on necromancy. Investing the goods with numinous importance was merely a matter of tapping into the buyer's reservoir of guilts and anxieties. The presence of those guilts and anxieties is the result of the gradual restructuring of the buyer's world view that this book has been following. It would seem that the consumer personality is in part a matter of information-routing in the brain. At times of decision those rational objective critical faculties that have given us our reputation as a commonsensical people are either overruled or bypassed.

Adman Tony Schwartz, in his book *The Responsive Chord*, argues that for a campaign to be an effective selling device, it must make the object being sold *resonate* in some way with the experience of the buyer. However, the resonances need not have anything to do with the prosaic nature of the object being sold. Rather, the resonances serve to bind an association between something good or pleasant and the item in question. Or, alternatively, the campaign might set up resonances so that the item becomes a way of avoiding something unpleasant or frightening, as in the case of Schwartz's famous anti-Goldwater TV spot which showed a girl picking flowers against a backdrop of a nuclear explosion. This idea of resonance is what we have been discussing in detail in the case of encyclopedia sales and the Wallace campaign, and in macrocosm in the instance of fads and outlaw cultural movements. It indicates that the floodgates that have impounded our irrational selves have been opened slightly, allowing some of those exiled contents to spill into daily life. As I have noted, when allowed expression these contents supersede reason. They involve archaic links to the command centers of the brain and generally take the form of an urgent need to act in some way. Reason might risk releasing this power, for it effectively circumscribes the choices of action to which this urgency might become attached. But what opens the floodgates?

Some word or other stimulus encountered triggers the release of the energy. Such an association might be the product of the consumer's experience, or it might be the product of some outside agency's attempt to associate a certain stimulus with the consumer's experience. In any event, latent in the consumer is the need to invest the desiccated world around him with charisma, and once that association is made, what we have is really the equivalent of the magician's "word of power." Once triggered, the consumer is engendered with a need, varying in intensity, to seek or, in some cases, avoid whatever stimulus is associated with that word. And as the previous chapters have tried to show, if at first this step does not involve a purchase of some sort, it soon will. Thus, this religious energy is brought back into the embrace of reason. The purchase, or vote, is a consummatory ritual. It precipitates the energy that builds when the association is triggered or educed. The world resumes its normal shape. The consumer returns to dormancy until he or she is again triggered into action.

These words might give the impression that there is something automatic about the consumer's performance. This is not the case. Rather, what I have been trying to show is that the increasing control of reason over our lives and the concomitant frustrations of our natural "religious" impulses have produced a set of predispositions that are common to the preponderance of the' population. During childhood we are imbued—whether we are academically successful or not—with a categorical, rationalistic way of factoring the phenomena around us. I believe that this kind of education involves the imprinting of a novel method of assigning meaning to perceptual information. Throughout this book I have been describing reason as having "usurped" nature's authority over the interpretation of information. There is a neurology to these usurpations. This commonly shared way of looking at the world produces a commonly shared set of anxieties and frustrations. Finally, there is the interplay between these two elements and the gradually accumulated structures of society and the economy. Again there is nothing automatic about the response of the consumer in this mix of predispositions and circumstances, but the tendencies that flow from a society founded on materialism and self-definition have progressively narrowed the forms this interplay might take. Thus, if the consumer personality is a device that translates religious needs into material appetites, it takes that form only because in the aggregate things tend to work out that way.

I have purposely confined my treatment of this model of the sales decision. My interest has been to show how the properties of a sales decision integrate various forces at work in the consumer's mind, and secondarily how the sales decision can be generalized to apply to a panoply of individual and mass phenomena. There is a wealth of information on the ways in which advertisers attempt to develop associations in the average American between the purchase of various products and worldly success, happiness, and other basic yearnings. As mentioned earlier, Tony Schwartz, in *The Responsive Chord,* convincingly shows how the "work" of advertising is to find images that "resonate" with the buyer's experience. Jeffrey Shrank's book, *Snap, Crackle, and Popular Taste,* shows the myriad insidious ways in which corporate

America attempts to set up these "resonances" and control our choices once the buyer is stimulated to act. And I am sure that each of us, by examining our own experience, can produce a wealth of occasions on which our common sense has been suspended because of a message cleverly charged with emotional urgency. To lead off these confessions, I will testify that although on principle I oppose fast-food restaurants, I feel warmly towards the young, fun-loving people I see cavorting in McDonald's ads. Their diffidence and enthusiasm resonates with my memories of a number of bright moments. On the other hand, I have yet to suffer a Big Mac attack, and so, while I feel warmly towards the McDonald image, I have yet to be induced to sample the reality. That moment may not be far off. To return to the point, my interest in this chapter has been to take the archetypal sales decision and to suggest that it was prepared for by a long series of events in history and evolution, to suggest that each sales decision performs work in a struggle we may not be aware of, and finally, to show that the structure of this sales decision is so deeply embedded in the way the individual relates to the world that it describes a personality.

However, to stop here would be to fall short of explaining how a consumer society bonds these various personalities into an integrated system. Actually, it is the aggregate behavior of the consumer society that gives the best profile of the individual consumer personality. Consumer behavior is a religion that reshapes the world around it, and we have already commented on the broad nature of the religion as evidenced by the reshapings effected by the consumer's purchases. A somewhat more elusive problem is my contention that the consumer society is not merely the sum of aggregate consumer purchases, but that, in the nature of a culture, it appears to have a life of its own which selects to some degree the behaviors of the individual within the society.

To make this point let us examine some of the broad defenses of a consumer society and the ways by which it enlists the individual to man and maintain these defenses.

~ 9 ~

Managing Consciousness:
The Defenses of a Consumer Society

THE CONSUMER SOCIETY AS ORGANISM

I have been arguing that a consumer society is a device that allows reason to use mankind as its proxy on earth. The broad purpose of a consumer society is to implement and enhance the control and rational management of nature. The consumer has become a willing proxy in this endeavor as the result of a gradual cultural evolution that has produced a personality that views the world through a rational grid. This personality contains a reservoir of disenfranchised unconscious needs which form a consumer society's working capital used in this grand scheme of reconstruction. I have considered the structure of the purchases that tap this working capital. Now let us look at the more conscious mechanisms of the consumer society, for if a consumer society is shaped at a level inaccessible to and beyond the control of the individual consumer, it evolves in this way because of the conscious belief in certain myths, such as the myth of progress. This chapter will consider the conscious allegiances that bind the consumer to the consumer society, and, in so doing, examine the ways in which a consumer society defends itself as a whole.

Just as rational perturbations of natural processes set in motion forces that seek to redress these imposed imbalances, so economic and social perturbations produce similar counterreactions which must be rationalized to maintain the allegiance of the consumer. Put simply, the consumer society promises a multiplicity of benefits to mankind, but these benefits entail costs that put stresses on the social conscience of the society. The consumer society is founded on personal, political, and material progress, a growth ethic that often requires that the individual place his immediate self-interest before his concern for his fellowman. At the same time, our society retains its ideals, which include, for instance, concern for our fellows, particularly the disadvantaged. As a result, there are what Daniel Bell has termed cultural contradictions in capitalism. We have already discussed how the Reformation prepared the way for an ethic that allowed the individual to place his interests above those of his fellowman and still feel that he was acting in a godly manner. But this problem is not merely an individual problem. A democratic society must, in the words of the politicians, attempt to live up to its promises. The problem—and this is an axiom of this chapter—is that for either the individual or the society literally and stringently to honor its ideals would bring the consumer society to a shuddering halt. The American consumer society was not built on the adherence to the political and social ideals of the founding fathers; it was built on the promise of the future realization of those ideals. If there is to be entrepreneurial spirit, those values which are legacies from society's communal origins are going to have to take a beating. Society had to and still has to appear to honor those values without threatening the economic health of the system. This problem set the stage for another of the consumer society's illusionist feats. To introduce this idea let us look briefly at an example of such defenses which I have examined elsewhere in great detail.

CHARITY

The United States, with 5 percent of the world's population, consumes roughly 25 percent of the world's annually recovered resources. For a long time we have been unable to live on the not inconsiderable resources contained within our own borders. The pressure that has spread American industry throughout the world has been the pressure for profits, and, more particularly, the normal competitive pressure for growth in profits. This not only creates demand for new sources of raw materials, it produces a constant need for new markets. No one would argue that the international involvement of American business is motivated by altruism: witness the familiar cries of exploitation and economic imperialism that follow the progress of business through the Third World. Whether or not the average American consciously perceives or admits that his relative affluence has been historically related to the deprivation of others, there has been an unconscious acknowledgment of and adjustment to this circumstance evident in the charitable impulse. This was the subject of my previous book, *The Alms Race,* which examined the nature of the charitable impulse as manifest in the impact of voluntary aid overseas. Its relevance to a book on consumer behavior lies in the form the charitable impulse has taken in voluntary aid. The ways in which we have tried to "help" the undeveloped countries of the world provides a model for the ways in which the consumer society tends to its conscience without threatening its economic health.

In *The Alms Race,* I organized my analysis around the question of why so many projects, ostensibly designed to help a given group of people, seemed to go wrong, either because they did not produce the desired result or because they produced side effects that obviated whatever gains the projects might produce. After studying a variety of different types of aid and development projects in Africa, I argued that projects that made little sense, if analyzed as intended to aid the beneficiary, made a great deal of sense, if analyzed from the perspective of the ways in which they benefited the donor and donor society. In effect, the charitable impulse was turned into a tool of the consumer society.

This has happened as the result of a concatenation of utterly ordinary circumstances. In the years following World War II, almost all voluntary agencies moved from straight relief into development work. This occurred because with the end of the dislocations caused by the war these agencies, in normal bureaucratic fashion, began looking around for reasons to stay in business. They noted that there existed in the American people an enormous "need to give" (as it was put by one voluntary agency official), and felt that it would dishonor that virtue if CARE and their ilk folded their tents simply because they had fulfilled their original ambitions. Thus, at the same time that American diplomacy and American business were discovering that there was a big world beyond Europe, the voluntary agencies began to wonder whether instead of merely treating the symptoms they should be attacking the root causes of poverty. This set the stage for their entrance into development work, where attacking the root cause of poverty translated ultimately to "bringing the American way of life beyond where the pavement ends."

After examining various programs and position papers used by CARE in project development, I discovered that the analysis of the different situations CARE was likely to enter was entirely self-reinforcing. To CARE, the non-Western way of life was the root cause of poverty. CARE claims that it attempts to tailor its programs to local eccentricities, but essentially CARE's debate about the best way to intervene in a given situation reverberates solely among alternatives within the consumer world view. There is no possibility for consideration of cultural values of the areas in which they work except as impediments to development. From a relief agency, CARE became an economic missionary spreading the faith, and through its projects, helped to lay the groundwork for the development of Western industry and values.

The argument made to justify development work is the same argument made about efforts to help the poor in the United States. It is: the poor are disadvantaged not by the system, but because they are not part of the system. Putting aside that defining what is poor is a difficult problem when one is working outside one's own society, this formulation touches on one of the central defenses of a consumer society, namely, that such problems as occur will be solved by the further extension of a pyramid sales scheme. Customer disaffections are co-opted by turning the victim into a salesman in search of new victims. This disguises for a time the fact that someone is left holding the bag. But more importantly, it transforms critical energy into a force abetting the object of criticism.

Few would argue that the charitable impulse in the United States is not partly fueled by the desire to expiate the sin of affluence. It represents the recognition that the consumer society is a pyramid sales scheme. Charitable giving provides a necessary safety valve for these potentially dangerous qualms. For a mere fraction of our gains we can straighten out our moral bookkeeping. But more than this, the form that giving takes serves as an argument for the intrinsic good of the system that provided wealth in the first place. Finally, the actual work performed by charitable giving often serves to fuel the economy by providing and opening new markets for American products, by improving the infrastructure necessary for future investment, and by helping to prepare and improve the labor market. Thus, an impulse that traces its origins to the communal bonds of our tribal past has been subtly altered until it has become a force in the fracturing of those bonds in societies where they still persist.

ENVIRONMENT

There are several other potentially troublesome threats to the consumer society which derive from its contradictions. These threats also are domesticated in a fashion similar to the process of co-optation just described for the charitable impulse. The remainder of this chapter will introduce several such problems. For instance, there is a threat posed by pollution and the degradation of the environment that results from our management and consumption of natural resources.

I have suggested that pollution and environmental degradation are the inevitable by-products of a consumer society. The consumer society views the environment as a collection of raw materials put on earth for our use. This analysis, which has guided our interventions in nature, is in fundamental discord with its subject matter. In this posture we could not help but defile the world around us. Besides, what were we defiling?

Wastelands . . . wilderness . . . idle resources. Traditionally, it is only when the environmental movement focuses on the threats pollution poses to our own health that it has serious and broad-based support. Environmentalist Gary Soucie points out that one of the earliest antipollution laws was a death sentence imposed for open burning enacted during a pollution crisis in medieval London. As one moves farther from issues that affect man's immediate health and safety, support for environmental issues narrows drastically unless the issue involves preservation for use by sportsmen. The idea that some of our natural surroundings ought to be protected, not because of their recreational or industrial utility to man, but because some of nature ought to be left to her own management has growing but relatively weak support.

These attitudes are now changing. In the terms we have been using, these attitudes are changing because the mind, having implemented its changes at the expense of the world around us, now finds that further changes must be effected at the expense of our own bodies. Ever more frequently, the price of increased affluence is our health. The scenario I projected earlier in the book, which suggested that the mind's ultimate victory over nature is suicide, is now a literal possibility.

This possibility is one of the fears that informs the environmental movement. Large numbers of people are beginning to notice that increases in the standard of living lead to decreases in the "quality of life." Even so, the response to this realization has been mixed. In Minnesota and Ohio, workers were violently against the closing or even modification of plants that posed health dangers in the form of air and water pollution. In these and similar cases the judgment seems to be that an immediate loss of pay is more onerous than the less visible and less immediate threat to their health. However, a far larger number of people, who do not yet feel the environmental movement as an economic threat, have pushed for legislation to protect the environment and abate pollution. Beyond this, there was a strong element of environmentalism and anticonsumer-society sentiment in the counterculture, which was a force demanding more radical steps than the legislation of tolerances for pollution and safeguards for the environment. This group recognized the fundamental incompatibility of a consumer society and nature, and advocating a form of pantheism, many attempted to quit the consumer society entirely and return to the land. As the chapter on Tahiti tried to point out, such gestures only served to underscore the difficulty of leaving or altering a consumer society.

Still, the environmental movement does pose a threat to our consumer society. It is a profound threat, because the consumer society is for the most part founded on waste and pollution. American industry recognizes this and industry leaders, such as Reginald Jones of General Electric, regularly target the environmentalists as the greatest threat to America's economic health. I believe that environmentalism and the antipodal world view it involves will prove to be the most enduring threat to the consumer society (and consequently our greatest hope for the future), but again, as in the case of the charitable impulse, it is interesting to follow the ways in which the consumer society has deflected and attempted to domesticate this threat to its "health". The more long-term changes signaled by environmentalism will be discussed later.

Like the counterculture, which saw itself as an army dedicated to the dismantling of the consumer society and ended as a boom-and-bust growth industry, the energy of the environmental movement has so far been more of a boon than a threat to the economic heart of the consumer society. This reformist energy has produced an entirely new growth industry. Where this energy might have taken the form of an assault on the sources of the problems, it has rather emerged in a janitorial capacity concerned with cleaning up the mess by applying the same technological and managerial methods that caused it. "Technology got us into this mess; it will get us out." The environmental movement as manifest in the creation of an industry devoted to sewage treatment, effluent recovery, air scrubbers, emission-control devices, and the like, has created more jobs than it has cost. The costs of this industry are borne by the taxpayers, by the consumer through higher prices, and by the dirtier industries that have been forced by law to clean up. It is easy to judge who benefits from environmental initiatives by who has complained the least. The chemical industry, one of the prime villains of the environmentalists, has benefited because it has the expertise to clean up and profit from its own mess. The steel and power companies, who have the most direct relationship between profits and restrictions on pricing, complain the loudest. Still, that the environmental movement means jobs and profits has been its major selling point to American business. It also indicates that another threat has been co-opted.

Up to a point there is a communality of interests between business and the environmentalists. If wastes or by-products can be sold or recycled, a minus is turned into a plus on the company's books. If regulations concerning pollution produce a new market for new goods, to a degree both the environment and business benefit. But this expansion of business activity can only exacerbate the dissonance between management and technology on the one hand, and nature on the other. The production of pollution-control equipment entails environmental costs of its own. Then there are the residual environmental effects produced by the profits and wages that result from this new market. The workers will in all likelihood use their wages to fuel the environmentally flawed consumer economy, helping to spread the disease their industry is supposed to help cure. In my long prolegomenon to the advent of a consumer society, I tried to show that the environmental problems we face derive ultimately from our posture toward nature. Any attempt to solve the "environmental crisis" that comes from that same posture and helps to expand or strengthen the ambit of that attitude toward nature can only compound rather than cure our environmental problems.

That society has chosen to confront the problems of pollution by attempting to clean up the mess rather than change the source is a perfectly natural consequence of our immense economic, political, and emotional investment in the philosophy of growth and progress. The clean-up approach enables us to retain our belief in technology. More immediately, it enables us to retain our jobs and profits, and it enables us to believe that we are confronting the environmental problems head on. In this last capacity, the cleanup approach provides an enormous service to the consumer society because it sops up an enormous amount of energy that if not accommodated might fuel a radical critique of society. This brings us to a critical defense mechanism of consumer societies, namely, the role of government and the role of bureaucracy.

The process by which the radical (in the sense that it represented a critique of the premises of a consumer society) energy of the environmental movement was domesticated is the political correlative to the process of domestication I described of the outlaw energy of the rock-music scene. As noted in the chapter on the consumer decision, the political expression of the frustrations innate in a consumer society can take several forms. Where it does surface in unalloyed radical form, it tends (on both the left and the right) to express itself through the theater of the rally rather than the real-life drama of the voting booth. But outbreaks of this energy have their effects on the mainstream of politics. Indeed, if it were not for this elastic responsiveness in our political machinery, the extremes might precipitate more violently and far reachingly than through theater. In this manner "kooks" signal the directions of the main political currents. They relate to the whole of the system in the way that fads relate to the economic heart of the consumer society. Some reflect evanescent constituencies, while others indicate broadly shared anxiety. The way such energy is politically assimilated indicates the responsiveness of our political system.

The selective processes of American politics have shaped the politician into a montage of the concerns and special interests of his constituency. The successful candidate must express his constituents' concerns without threatening entrenched economic powers. The politician becomes a device which mediates between the potentially disruptive concerns awash in the voters and the basic structures of the consumer society. As such he must be able to attach himself to the abatement of such anxieties as affect his constituency, but whatever abatement he promises must be acceptable to the differently weighted interests that produced those anxieties. In California, Governor Jerry Brown has been cited as the paradigm for these protean abilities: creating the impression of emotional resonance with the voiced and unvoiced needs of Californians, while acting legislatively in a relatively conservative manner. This is the basic function of the elected official: to feel radically, but to act conservatively. It was summed up perfectly by the Nixon aide who said, "Watch what we do, not what we say."

What most elected politicians do is legislate, and because of the pressures acting on the political process, remedial legislation—the carrying out of campaign promises to deal with some constituent concern—often has a larger symbolic importance than remedial capability. The legislative process is not so much concerned with effecting change as it is with abating the anxieties that produce the desire for change. It is this point that ties together the individual consumer personality and the total behavior of the consumer society, and, because of its importance, I will devote a good deal of the remainder of this book to its discussion.

The environmental movement has produced many examples of this genre of legislation. For instance, in California, environmentalists put a referendum on the ballot that would prohibit the construction of any future power plants unless they could be guaranteed completely safe. The power industry was united in opposition to this referendum because they felt that there was no way the safety of power plants could be guaranteed. On the other hand, they did not want to *say* that. After avoiding the issue as long as he could, Governor Jerry Brown offered the compromise of establishing a review board to examine construction plans for all new power plants. This, of course, did not offer the safety guarantees the referendum required, but it assuaged voter fears sufficiently to co-opt most of the support that would otherwise have gone to passing the referendum. This pattern of gradually dampening oscillation between militant environmentalists and the interest groups affected has characterized much of the approach to environmental problems at the federal as well as the state level. The pattern is for a somewhat toothless piece of legislation to be offered as a viable compromise. The environmentalist is left with a feeling of accomplishment, the public concern is assuaged, and the source of the problem is either unaffected or only lightly stung.

And there are now agencies to administer such legislation at the federal, state, and even city levels. This is a phenomenon that follows quickly in the wake of the detection of a problem, just as a corporate superstructure quickly caps outbreaks of consumer interest. We might consider briefly the genesis of one such federal bureaucracy as an example of how the consumer society manages political and social discontent. The Environmental Protection Agency which administers such laws at the federal level was created out of President Nixon's Government Reorganization Plan No. 3, and was authorized by the House in September of 1970. Nixon proposed the EPA in part to forestall Congress foisting it on him. The idea was to have an agency, independent of the pressures of special interests and of the interests of the other cabinet offices, solely concerned with protecting the environment. The EPA has vigorously honored this mandate; however, this does not mean that the United States had successfully dealt with its environmental problems. For one thing, Congress has the power to change the standards that the EPA administers, and when clean has become too expensive Congress has weakened its own legislation. Secondly, the EPA has institutionalized and given tremendous weight to the flawed approach to environmental problems that we have been discussing. It has done this simply because it is in the self-interest of those who work for EPA to endorse this approach to environmental problems.

There has been some theoretical debate about the proper approach to environmental problems, for instance, whether in the case of air pollution the government should set standards for the quality of the air or whether it should control pollution at the source by taxing industries and individuals according to their contribution to polluting the environment. As Charles

Schultz has pointed out in *The Public Use of Private Interest,* such taxes could be scaled to the prohibitive for truly dangerous pollutants. That this second approach has not been adopted is because it gives government less to do. A lesson that has finally come home to the American public—as various tax initiatives and referenda indicate—is that there is no constituency in government for any legislation that seeks to lessen its role, while there is an enormous interest in any regulatory or administrative approach to problems that will enhance the size of government. We will address the question of government as a special interest group in a moment. With regard to the EPA it should be obvious that those working for that body will endorse an approach to environmental problems that will give them the most possible power.

What I have been trying to show here is that when the consumer society produces problems such as pollution, it has mechanisms to turn to its own purposes the reformist energy produced by the consciousness of those problems. The process by which a radical critique of society has its effect on law is a process by which government, through its response to this critique, gradually narrows the alternatives such reforms might take until what was once a jolt at the heart of the consumer society becomes a debate about alternatives entirely within the ambit of the consumer society. Thus, although a radical critique may still be justified, most of the energy that would support it has been abated by the superficial appearance of having dealt with the problem. Finally, the solutions adopted harness this energy to the advantage of the consumer society, first, by creating new markets for new industries, and second, by enhancing the power of government. As in the case of the individual, this consumer mechanism "solves" the problem posed in the *Bacchae.* Government expands its hegemony over the lives and resources of the populace in the precise manner I have described for reason's expansion of its hegemony over new behaviors; but government not only benefits from the problems it creates (which demand more government programs to set things right), it also expands its power as the problems attendant to a consumer society expand. The size of government is a living metaphor for the growing role of reason in managing our lives. This is no coincidence.

Bureaucracy is the most concrete measure of the size of any government. We have been discussing the creation of one new bureaucracy—the EPA— and the forces that have added layers of equivalent bureaucracy at the state and city level. Since the environmental crisis produced the EPA, we have also seen the energy crises produce the Department of Energy. Moreover, crises that do not demand new cabinet offices often produce departments within existing bureaucracies. Thus, the spreading of drug abuse produced the Drug Enforcement Agency under the Justice Department, while smaller or more transitory issues produce presidential commissions or congressional committees. The nature and behavior of bureaucracies has been the subject of much study and much humor. It has been written that their first instinct is self-perpetuation, that they have a conserving relationship with their subject matter, that they breed out initiative and innovation, and that given a choice between effectiveness and administrative clarity, a bureaucracy will always choose an approach that is administrable. Indeed, there can be little argument that the organizational constraints of a bureaucracy must inevitably bleed the vigor out of a desire to solve some problem. I believe that this is the precise purpose of bureaucracy in a consumer society. That is, bureaucracies do not exist to solve problems, but rather to abate the anxiety that problems exist which are not being solved. In this capacity they act like a psychic sponge—they absorb and thus abate energy that might otherwise take more militant expression.

The militancy of the environmental movement ends up defused and domesticated in the EPA. A large part of the population who were roused by anxieties about pollution can now return to complacency, secure in the belief that the EPA is looking after the environment for them. And indeed, since the establishment of the EPA, environmentalists have been having a hard time rousing the public about environmental problems that continue to be generated by the consumer society. In large part managing problems like pollution, which are bound up with the prosperity of a consumer society, is managing the consciousness of these problems.

This is something that the politicians who establish new bureaucracies are well aware of. To call for the establishment of a new department or bureau is to make a dramatic gesture which communicates to the voters that this is a candidate who is going to do something about X. The establishment of the department, whether or not it solves X, permits the voters to go back to sleep. This process is like the syndrome that character-izes the investment my victim would make in an encyclopedia to buy back the complacency disturbed by the properties of the sales pitch: the money we invest as taxpayers in the various bureaucracies we have established to deal with our pressing problems buys us release from these problems. On both the individual level and the governmental level the essence of this system is "containment" not solution. Just as the buyer is forever susceptible to the manipulation of those fundamental anxieties attendant to the consumer personality, so are we as a nation ever susceptible to new eruptions of the fundamental social and environmental problems that are by-products of the affluence of the consumer society.

MANAGING THE CONSCIOUSNESS OF PROBLEMS

Another such problem is crime, a by-product of a consumer society, but perennially regarded as unnecessary and soluble. Of course I do not mean to imply that crime appeared with the advent of consumer behavior. What I want to suggest here is that certain types of crime are inevitable if society is to free the entrepreneurial spirit, and that crime like pollution is a problem consumer societies manage rather than solve. In a change-oriented society what is legal and what is illegal is somewhat removed from the immediate, emotionally rein-forced absolutes that govern a steady-state society. Often what is legal and illegal is subject to change. When the agent of change in such a society is entrepreneurial activity, there must be some spillover between sanctioned and unsanctioned entrepreneurial activity. Necessary to it is the promotion of one's self-interest as a paramount occupation and a concomitant subordination of communal responsibilities to the promotion of self-interest. With the fracturing of the moral force of those ties, there is little to prevent the individual from pursuing whatever course will most directly satisfy his needs. As we well know, the state is not nearly as good an enforcer of rectitude as is the belief in an avenging god. What has prevented a total descent into chaos is that most people value the good opinion of their family and neighbors. Consequently, most people seek to justify their actions, if not legally, through appeal to some extralegal justifying principle such as political or economic repression. If there is a community tolerant of activities ostensibly illegal, such as drug dealing, there is little the state can do other than contain the activity.

The structural differences between legal and illegal entrepreneurial activity are not always great. A salesman might console himself that a family might be better off owning their unwanted set of books, but, as I discovered, in many cases the structure of the sale is such that the product to be delivered is less important than the sale itself. Selling the Great Books, which some would say was laudable, was no different from selling the New Standard Encyclopedia, which should have been illegal. The entrepreneur is insulated from the consequences of his activity by the thrill of the activity itself and the dog-eat-dog ethic of a consumer society. After selling encyclopedias I could easily understand how the momentary satisfactions of success in that field might lead an honest man into dishonesty. In the amoral world of sales, the only thing that prevents one from straying beyond the tolerances that define the difference between the legal and illegal are fears of social and legal consequences. If one is working outside of one's community, or if one's community tolerates what the law will not, there is only the uncertain force of the law. The rationale that the entrepreneur is servicing a need permits him to retain an air of self-righteousness even when he does run afoul of the law. Nor should we be surprised to find this same self-righteousness among pimps, racketeers, and drug dealers. The problem of fulfilling one's ambitions is compounded in ghetto life where often the traditional opportunities for the entrepreneur are in activities that are illegal across the board.

If I have been focusing on the contradictions in the entrepreneurial spirit, it is because this spirit is the main creative energy of a consumer society. Most of the major corporations in America were entrepreneurial in their beginnings. However, the attitudes manifest in the entrepreneur occur in varying degree in a far larger segment of the population. A corporate executive might attempt to conceal or minimize the carcinogenic properties of his product and at the same time feel contempt for the ethics of the drug dealer. This may seem like hypocrisy, but it should be clear that it is quite natural behavior within the terms of society in which the connection between act and responsibility has been purposefully fudged.

What this means is that our prosperity is as surely tied to crime as it is to pollution. This, in turn, means that the consumer society must once again contain a problem while at the same time appearing to attempt to eradicate it. Again, as in the case of pollution, the outrage that derives from the consciousness of crime has been harmlessly diverted down false alleyways, and away from a potentially damaging critique of the structure of consumer behavior. Crime, which in our case is closely tied to our affluence, has been approached against all evidence as though it were a function of poverty. Moreover, debate has naturally focused on the more violent crimes and the element of violence in crime which serves to obscure a substrate of criminality of which violence is but a small part.

Even with crimes of violence, the incidence of crime is at best marginally affected by the money spent on law enforcement. We might use the example to illustrate the conserving relationship between agencies and the problems they manage. In New York City, the incidence of violent crimes bears almost a direct relationship to the size of the police force, rising as the police force became larger during the sixties and early seventies, and then falling at the time that budgetary constraints were forcing reductions of police manpower.

Of all the problems innate in a consumer society, crime is the problem whose bonds with our nature has been most often acknowledged. Most people regard crime and corruption as part of human nature, a view that is only too readily confirmed by the most casual perusal of the daily newspapers. And with the exception of a declining number of humanistic, liberal thinkers, most people consciously think of crime as something to be contained rather than eradicated. Thus, few people ask why, after numerous wars on drugs, organized crime, or government corruption, we still have all three. Crime is possibly the only issue where the public consciously expects nothing more than that government *seem* to try to root it out. Testimony to this equipoise is that outrage quickly surfaces when someone or some group violates our unstated tolerance for criminality, for instance, in crimes that involve the elderly or minors, or crimes that embody some deep fears, such as the Manson slayings, which tapped the projected guilts of the consumer society. In such cases people demand something more than the appearance of trying, and it is instructive how effective law enforcement agencies can be when tackling crimes, once criminals are stripped of their protection by various interests.

EDUCATION

I have been arguing that the relationship of the nation to its discontents replicates that of the individual. To elucidate this connection, let us look at how we are selected to play out different roles in this drama as it occurs at the societal level. In general, we are sorted into our different societal roles during childhood, and on the basis of how well we react to being forced into the confining categories of American education. Education is another area of a consumer society where a system that appears to be plagued with solvable problems actually is functioning as it is supposed to function to fulfill the requirements of the consumer society. If we look at American education according to the needs of a consumer society, rather than from the perspective of liberal ideals, we can see that many of the supposed failures of education are successes.

For instance, a great preponderance of the entrepreneurs and innovators are often either academic failures or academically indifferent. There are exceptions of course—like Edwin Land, of Polaroid, whose academic talents got him into Harvard—but the archetypal American genius in business or science has his success in spite of attempts by schools or his superiors to suffocate his spirit. These attempts at suffocation are a necessary part of the entrepreneur's motivations. Success and vindication are his revenge for the insults of his youth. Essential to the chemistry that creates entrepreneurs are insensitive, rote-minded teachers and confining restrictions. In this respect the American educational system is an outstanding success. But those petty restrictions that fire the hatred of the entrepreneur have other useful functions as well. To illustrate one such function, let us examine a particular problem that would seem to be soluble and yet has continued to worsen despite repeated official efforts to solve it. The problem is literacy.

Ever since Jefferson wrote that the best defense of a democracy is an informed electorate, universal literacy has been viewed as key to the health of the republic. An illiterate electorate is a pawn in the hands of interpreters. As the electorate has been democratized to include almost everybody, so too have the goals of literacy expanded to universality. Universal literacy is not a controversial issue. No vested interest states that it will lose should everybody be able to read. Furthermore, learning to read is the easiest intellectual exercise there is. Caleb Gattegno—the well known expert on child education—says that the intellectual ability necessary to learn to read is so rudimentary that "any child who has learned to speak has developed the mental powers necessary to learn to read." Yet, Gattegno is regarded as a miracle worker merely because he has demonstrated this fact. Today, after sixty years of effort toward achieving what has been, since the birth of the nation, a national goal, and after the expenditure of tens of billions of dollars on various primary and remedial reading programs, over 40 percent of the nation's school children cannot read effectively, and more than half the adult population is hobbled because of semiliteracy. Moreover, these figures have remained fairly steady over the past few decades. Even the most primitive society manages to teach its children what is necessary to survive in their environment. Because there is no apparent opposition to literacy, what we can conclude from our failure to impart this basic skill is that it is not a basic skill. Although we may idealize universal literacy, perhaps it is not in the best interests of a consumer society to achieve it. Perhaps the failures of American education are necessary to the economy and the consumer society. There are, of course, a host of explanations for the declining literacy of Americans: for instance, the development of television, affluence, or the neglect of minorities. All of these factors affect literacy to some degree. However, I would suspect that these factors have their effects on a norm that is not universal literacy, but rather on a base of about 40 percent that our culture has determined is an appropriate level of literacy for the society as a whole.

The world view that is the foundation of the consumer personality is stamped on the young during education, and it is so critically important to the functioning of a consumer society that I would be inclined to look at even the most aggravating insensitivities of the educational system as purposeful, just as I would be inclined to view its failures as purposeful. Education is the area in which the individual is first forced to adapt to the standards and categories of a rationally managed society, and the student's reactions to these forms determine to some degree what role he will play in that society. I have already mentioned the entrepreneur as someone who in all likelihood unsuccessfully adapted to such rigors, but this kind of failure characterizes an extremely small percentage of the population. On the other hand, the resentments and motives that such an unsuccessful adaptation breeds apply to far greater numbers of people who do not become entrepreneurs.

Schools, of course, vary radically in curriculum and student body composition. I would note that the institutional aspects of schooling have for the consumer society an educational importance that is broader, and perhaps more important, than any variations in curriculum. Throughout this chapter we have been discussing various ways in which institutional structures impose their own organization on their subject matter and how, on occasion, bureaucratic exigencies have more weight than an organization's avowed purpose. Institutions have more power than individual teachers have inspiration.*

Most students, even successful ones, quickly forget the particular details of their education. Some learn a method of problem-solving in different disciplines, but almost all learn that the forms of schooling are more important than the substance. Both genius and stupidity are penalized. Recognition of the authority of the institution and its forms is rewarded. As such, our schooling system is a sorting device for the individual's role in society. It is the first point at which the irrationally based individual meets the rationally based structures of society. Those who adapt the forms and standards of their schooling ultimately take their place in the managerial ranks of the public and private sector. Those who fail to master the forms and the subject matter are the nation's labor force. Recall that when I sold encyclopedias, I summoned memories of my buyer's failure to measure up to society's standards as the most persuasive tool in the sales pitch.

Society needs these workers and it needs its obedient buyers

---

*A nice example of this phenomenon occurred in New York a couple of years ago when teachers prepared students for standardized reading programs by helping them to memorize the answers. The student, in this instance, was reduced to a nettlesome pawn who stood in the way of a bureaucracy fulfilling its own purposes. For their part, the teachers had more fear of not satisfying the group-level performance requirements of the test than they had desire to teach their pupils to read. Within the system, the pupils were less important than their scores. This is not a lesson that is lost on students.

of consumer goods. It needs the failures of the educational system as much as it needs the successes. The institutional aspects of education guarantee that the supply of such people will continue, regardless of the amount of money thrown at the "national disgrace" of illiteracy.

I have attempted to show that the ways in which the consumer society as a whole tries to solve its intrinsic social problems and satisfy the idealism of its constituents parallel the ways in which the consumer society capitalizes on its discontents as they surface culturally. Both these broad patterns of response reflect, in macrocosm, the patterns that determine the individual's relationship to the world. This is to say, as in the case of the individual purchase, our public purchases are educed and molded by powerful anxieties rather than the practical exercise of common sense. A difference is that while each encyclopedia sale would enhance the profits of the private company, each new purchase of government programs enhances the power of government. Which brings us to the final tumbler in the structure of consumer societies and the subject of the next chapter. If the relationship between government and the endemic problems of a consumer society is conserving, the growth of government has a very real purpose in the evolutionary battle we have been following.

~ 10 ~

Reason's Proxy: Government

THE ROLE OF GOVERNMENT

Throughout the preceding chapters, discussion of consumer behavior has returned to the basic theme in which eruptions of energy and anxiety lead to the expansion of a structure of management entirely opposite in spirit to the nature of the energy it capitalizes on. This description perfectly describes the political evolution of the United States. Founded on a renegade distrust of governments, and graced with a Constitution artfully designed through checks and balances to foil the tendencies of those in power to increase their hold over the people, the United States is now suffocating under the weight of ever-larger accretions of government at all levels. We tend to look to our libertarian roots for an expression of what America is all about, just as economically we would hold up the self-made man or entrepreneur as the objective of our system. However, if we look at the nature of a consumer society, we can see that this is not the case. Although I have devoted a large part of this book to discussing the cultural events that freed the entrepreneurial spirit, the purpose of freeing that spirit was not to create a race of pioneers, but rather to effect a radical restructuring of the environment and society. These restructurings, which eventually suffocate the entrepreneurial spirit and political freedom, are what a consumer society is all about. What we regard as the creative heart of our society is merely the tool of society to effect these changes. It testifies to the power of myth that we should

157

regard the increasing regimentation of life a mystifying by-product of circumstances not at all connected to the heart of our society, while in reality they are the very goal of society. Like the Maring in New Guinea, we are tricked by our "ancestors"—our culture—into performing functions we do not understand. Let us take a look at these tricks as they are evident in the role of government.

The trend toward more government most directly mirrors the increase in the role of reason in managing human affairs and the environment. As reason replaced religion and tradition in the United States as the tissue which binds communities, governs commerce, and organizes behavior, it was inevitable that power would accrue to government as arbiter of law and standards, even though a quite real characteristic of the American people was distrust of government and the celebration of individual liberties. In the last chapter we examined some of the pressures that led to the expansion of government and its attendant bureaucracy as well as some of the "services" government provides. What was perhaps obscured by the thrust of that argument is that whatever psychological or mythic basis this process may have, the legacy of the public's investment in government is a very real increase in the power of government to control the behavior of individuals. Government increases in size in response to the salesmanship of politicians who adroitly tap commonly shared anxieties to install themselves in office. However, long after the politician is in office and the issue that has propelled him there has dropped (perhaps temporarily) from immediate consciousness, there remain his or her "programs" which in all likelihood may have quite a different influence on our lives from what the voters thought they were purchasing. Quite often this takes the form of standards or guidelines or specifications—for the fire-resistance of fabrics, or the hiring and firing of blacks, women, and other minorities, or for any of the other myriad aspects of private life where there is the potential for fraud, discrimination, or health hazards. And quite often such interference has little meaning or substance other than the exercise of authority.

We see this time and again: tragedies occur—a grain storage bin explodes, for instance, which leads Congress to mandate codes or standards, which in turn produce forms which are filled out and forgotten until a new tragedy occurs because of a lack of enforcement. Then the whole cycle begins again. However, behind the seeming meaninglessness of this cycle is the substantive change of giving the government an "option" to exert authority over an expanding range of human activities, an option that contains the threat that it might be exercised at any time. The purpose of the red tape we associate with a constricting bureaucracy is to maintain the visibility of that option and to enforce conformity in human affairs. That red tape often has no regulatory effect is not so important as the fact that it constantly reasserts the supremacy of reason as the arbiter of human affairs.

Each new area of behavior that is brought within the government's purview also increases the government's call on one's earnings. This, of course, brings ever-increasing percentages of national income under management. If frustrations about the government's increased meddling in the shaping of human behavior produced inarticulate, inchoate frustrations, such as those projected in the Wallace movement, the government's increasing claim on income to finance this meddling has reached a threshold where it has produced a much more potent expression of political outrage in the form of referenda and tax initiatives. While in the late 1960s there was no political constituency for anything more than a theatrical attack on the cult of reason, in the late 1970s the same frustrations that fueled the Wallace movement's anti-government, anti-intellectual aspects have now resurfaced. The frustrations that fed the so-called tax revolt are quite similar to those that invigorated the Wallace movement, but the constituency is much broader, and the form in which these frustrations have surfaced permits the voters to express palpably their frustrations through a vote, without directly asserting that they wish to abandon the services they perceive that government provides. The tax initiative or referendum permits the voter to say that he is only voting to eliminate the bad parts—waste, inefficiency, corruption—in government, while still retaining his or her belief in the ultimate wisdom and good intentions of government programs. This at least has been the picture that has emerged from various profiles of the supporters of tax initiatives. But there is more to the tax revolt than the unresolved confusion of the voters with regard to their posture toward government. The tax revolt and the response of government focuses several of the forces shaping the role of government in a consumer society, and reveals several ironies as the political process attempts to assimilate an anxiety about big government, which is the product of the voters' anxieties about other problems.

Perhaps the greatest irony of the tax revolt is that the form it has taken (bypassing state legislatures through what is called direct democracy) indicates that a large segment of the population has come to the conclusion that their elected representatives are not to be trusted with the issue of taxes. This is an astonishing development in a nation that grew out of a tax revolt and that was founded upon the notion of representation. On the other hand, we should not be surprised if citizens again decide to take matters into their own hands after decades of electing officials who promise to lower taxes and instead, raise them. This implied distrust of elected representatives indicates a crack in American idealism, which in turn may mean that the relationship between the public and government is changing. The tax revolt indicates that there is the beginning of a recognition by the voters that no matter what constituency elects a politician, once elected he or she crosses an invisible line in which the politician's new constituency is government. This seductiveness of power was recognized by the framers of the Constitution who did everything possible to keep such temptations out of reach. In devising the Constitution, the states were chary of ceding taxing power to the federal government without qualifying the government's power to levy a direct tax so that this power could not be used in a confiscatory way. Fresh in their minds was their experience with the Stamp Act, of which Franklin wrote, "it is intended to extort money from us, or ruin us by the consequences of refusing to pay" (Parliamentary History). To that end, the Constitution specifies that "it [Congress] must impose direct taxes by the rule of apportionment, and indirect taxes by the rule of uniformity." The principles of uniformity and apportionment would prevent the stronger states from ganging up on the weaker. A reading of *Pollock* v. *Farmer's Loan & Trust Co.*, the 1894 decision in which the income tax was declared unconstitutional, reveals that there was a general apprehension about giving Congress the right to levy direct taxes at all. This was allayed with reassurances that this power would be exercised as a last resort, and that through apportionment the states would retain the ability to check the power of the federal government.

In fact, this check worked, as evidenced by the fact that the Supreme Court struck down the income tax law of 1894 by which Congress sought to employ what was regarded as an extraordinary means of taxation during peacetime—without honoring the principle of apportionment according to representation. The government, however, having glimpsed the potential of this source of revenue was not to be put off by some nettlesome stumbling block like the Constitution, and ultimately in 1913 this impediment to growth was removed with the sixteenth amendment.* With its passage, the balance of power in the United States shifted irrevocably in favor of the federal government and allowed the tremendous growth of the federal budget which has characterized this century, a growth that has occurred in peacetime as well as wartime, and, since the discovery of stimulus spending, has even been immune to recession. While Congress fully recognizes its responsibilities to spend more than it takes in during recessions, it has conveniently forgotten that the other side of the coin is that it is supposed to recoup these deficits by restraining spending and running a surplus during times of prosperity. Thus, government spending has now freed itself from the limitations of economic growth.

*The Congress shall have power to lay and collect taxes on incomes from whatever source derived, without apportionment among the several States, and without regard to any census or enumeration.

The federal government now has to extend taxation hori-
zontally because marginal rates on income have reached a
level where (when considered with steeply rising claims on
income from states and municipalities) politicians sense the
dangers of an electoral uprising, massive evasion, and what is
called "disincentivation." Back when the income tax was
debated, opponents speculated about the nightmarish possibility that rates for the average man might reach 20 percent
(and were chastised for using scare tactics). Today the federal
government alone has a claim on 42 percent of national
income (as compared with 12 percent of national income in
1929). The combined burden of federal, state, and local taxes
have produced, to some degree, the effects described above.
Estimates of the underground economy—a cash economy
whose purpose is to evade taxes—range as high as $200 billion
annually. The tax revolt has politicians on the defensive and
economists regularly warn that the United States might reach
the stage approached by Britain where, increasingly, people
are refusing to seek or employ skills or professions because of
the disincentives of confiscatory rates of taxation.

Thus government is faced with the problem of financing its
growth without crossing the various flash points that are
beginning to appear in the economy and in the social fabric.
This pushes taxes into new frontiers—the informality that
marked the collection of capital-gains taxes on a host of
tangible appreciated assets is fast disappearing. But this
search for new income also surfaces in a couple of unlikely
and even paradoxical guises. One is tax reform; the other is
inflation.

It's easy for Congress to push tax relief for the poor simply
because the poor don't pay taxes. So argues Paul Craig
Roberts, a member of the United States Senate staff. The
lowest 50 percent of the taxpayers contribute only 7.1 percent
of the taxes paid. Thus, tax reform with its populist image of
getting the bloated rich is really an excuse for government to
go after the middle class. "Most people think that tax reform
means making the rich pay taxes," writes Roberts. "They do
not realize that the purpose of closing loopholes is to enlarge

the tax base by redefining personal income to include fringe benefits and capital gains and by reducing deductions." Roberts's point is that the government has nearly reached the limit of what it can take from the income of the highest brackets, and that the great new frontier is attacking what most would call the middle brackets. For instance, President Carter's tax reforms proposed on January 21, 1978, included proposals to tax unemployment benefits, and the elimination of such deductions as personal-property taxes and medical expenses—hardly loopholes for the rich. Moreover, argues Roberts, the government, through capital gains, now directly taxes real value in the manner of a wealth tax. Capital-gains taxes do not recognize inflation (although Carter's recent reduction of capital gains was a gesture in that direction), and by taxing appreciation without recognizing the increase in replacement value, tax reform taxes assets as income and thus confiscates assets—realizing the great fear of government that dominated the Constitutional Convention.

This brings us to inflation. Before discussing its utility to government let us take a look at its role in a consumer society. Inflation has been with us, the monetarists tell us, for 2,700 years—which makes it coeval with minted money. This indicates that it is hardly a problem unique to modern American life. Still, the very heart of a consumer society is inflationary. Our special brand of inflation occurs when the infinite ambitions for growth and progress meet the finite constraints and resources of the real world. An economist would say that inflation occurs when prices increase faster than purchasing power. Prices begin to increase faster than purchasing power when costs are added to the price of goods or services which do not in turn produce increases in productivity. For instance, increased wages without increased productivity, increased costs that reflect the environmental price of the product, increased costs of government and government services that erode purchasing power and push up prices (since such costs are passed on wherever possible), and increased world competition for basic resources of production: all of these factors are inflationary. In this sense, some of the recent inflationary costs have merely been discounting the cost of living to noneconomic costs and the declining situation of the United States as a world power. There is an irony in this last point, for the increased competition for resources throughout the world derives largely from our success in expanding the perimeter of the consumer society. Not too long after a society develops a demand for consumer goods, it is going to want to produce them itself. This in turn will change its posture with regard to buying finished goods from the United States and selling its resources to us. In this sense we can see that in the long term there are inflationary pressures within the very forces for growth. This point gets close to the heart of the relationship between inflation and a consumer society.

A certain measure of inflation is inevitable in a consumer society because with an ethos that believes in growth and progress, individual expectations will always run somewhat ahead of society's ability to realize them. Expectations will inevitably run ahead of whatever is realized. Technological advance may drop the price of some goods, such as calculators, computers, automobiles, and so on, but as long as people are looking upward that is where prices will go. Virulent inflation can be caused by excessive unproductive drains on the economy, such as the Vietnam war, which was largely financed by the inflation of the years following the war. But it can also be the product of a growth society finally approaching its limits either through the exhaustion of basic resources, the maturation of its technology, or the suffocation of its entrepreneurial and creative spirit. This seems to be our plight. A consumer society takes a posture toward the world that requires enormous and ever-increasing amounts of both physical and mental energy to maintain. Diminishing sources of energy and its concomitantly increasing cost tax our consumer society in several ways, the most evident of which is inflation. This inflation will be with us until there is some change in our expectations concerning growth and progress. That change, when it occurs, will not only spell the end of inflation, but of the consumer society as well.

Inflation helps government in several ways. Because of the progressive rate structure, people with no real increase in income or even a decline in real purchasing power can still end up paying more of their income in taxes. Moreover, as Roberts points out, inflation raises money without Congress having to legislate higher rates. The figure generally used is that a 10.5 rate of inflation produces a 16.5 percent increase in government revenues. Thus, while the average worker has kept pace with inflation over the past ten years, his spending power has declined because of his increased tax burden. If it is government spending that is producing inflation so much the better, because it is by its very profligacy that government finances its growth.

If this profligacy causes problems, better still. In his conclusions Roberts ascribes to government the same process of capitalizing on its own problems that I have described for the other functions of a consumer society:

> The advent of several major tax increases in tandem will destabilize the economy, but from the government's perspective that is desirable. There will have to be more government programs to deal with the consequence of instability. Every sophisticated person is aware of how special interests use the legislative process for their own benefits, but the same sophisticate is badly schooled in how the legislative process furthers the special interests of those in government. Inflation leads to the imposition of wage and price controls and credit allocation all of which increase the spoils, money and influence divvied up in Washington. Unemployment means more CETA jobs and public works, and what member of the government class is hurt by that? Put simply, instability increases the demand for the services of bureaucrats and for pork-barrel legislation that builds the spending constituencies of both Congress and the Executive branch. It advances the careers of academics and technocrats who move back and forth from their think tanks and universities and in and out of government.

Roberts's remarks touch on one of the practical forces that militates for ever-larger doses of government. Instability dealt with by government programs also creates jobs for the masses of degree-laden graduates who each year enter a job market with only a small number of openings in the private sector. Economist Jay Levy estimates that society could well get by with 10 percent of the number of college graduates we produce today. That we produce such a large surplus of graduates, especially in the liberal arts, reflects a societal judgment that the most worthwhile work is done with the intellect. The result of this judgment is that society produces a powerful constituency for the growth of government programs in this surplus of college graduates.

Given such innate forces for government growth, how would we expect the federal government to deal with the anxieties that are building about the uncontrolled growth of government and which are surfacing in the various tax initiatives? The California legislature and local governments responded to Proposition 13 by axing a host of programs designed to give funds to support summer schools, recreational programs, and other funded projects that might be sacrificed without touching the heart of the civil service. President Carter came into office an avowed enemy of government waste and saw himself in a holy war against the federal bureaucracy. His reforms have added to the size of the federal government and added new layers of red tape. His tax cut actually contains a tax rise, and federal spending continues to increase faster than real growth as indicated by the Gross National Product index. At local, state, and federal levels, none of the upheavals that were supposed to follow from the tax revolt have yet materialized. Even those initiatives that place limits on state spending still allow spending to grow. In essence, government seems to have the means to insulate itself against the will of the people even when the voters make their will directly known by passing what in a supreme irony has become government's first line of defense—representation.

It also should be clear that government takes the anxieties and aspirations of the people as a mandate for growth, but once growing, it is ruled by some other authority than the will of the people. This higher authority is reason, which seeks the rational management of society. In this regard government at all levels is essentially a mechanism for the development and imposition of formal standards of behavior. The purpose of a consumer society is first to unleash and then harness the energy necessary to effect this reorganization. That is why government keeps getting larger, and that is why it is no accident that this happens. The tax revolt indicates that this expansion is beginning to be felt. It also indicates that the people are relatively powerless to check this process. As I have argued throughout the book, this process is the filling out of a paradigm that dates to Hellenistic times. What we see happening at the national level in the relationship of government to people and their problems is merely a macrocosmic projection of the structure of the personality within a consumer society. Ultimately, both the individual and society as a whole seek order. The order we seek does not provide us with peace. Rather, it provides reason with a palpable expression of its authority over nature.

From this perspective we can see that there are strong similarities between the USSR and the United States. Both societies are regressing toward the same mean, although the USSR began with total management control and is working, mostly unofficially, toward the controlled release of entrepreneurial energy to fuel its economy. We, on the other hand, began with the unrestrained entrepreneur and are working toward the managed life. In both societies material aspirations have supplanted religion, leaving reason as the arbiter of social and individual worth. The Soviet Union, which is cumbersomely constructed around the economics of supply, misinterprets an essential element of a consumer society. That is that demand in a consumer society is the changeable emotional engine of a consumer society. The Soviets fail to see the religious substrate of the consumer purchase, although they worship material goods. Both the Soviets and Americans are pawns in reason's experiments with humanity and nature, experiments which in some ways recall the rhetoric of political campaigns. One of the most frequently used metaphors to describe unworkable programs or runaway bureaucracy is the

candidate's statement: "They have created a Frankenstein."*
The image is a more appropriate metaphor for the nature of
government and the nature of a consumer society than even
its most frequent users might like to think.

Mary Shelley's Dr. Frankenstein attempted to create life out
of bodily parts once their life was spent and the parts interred
in the grave. The doctor succeeded in this patchwork resur-
rection and his creation ultimately destroyed him. Mary
Shelley's creature has had a mythic hold on our imaginations
ever since. I think the power of the Frankenstein myth is that
it captures the dark side of the myth of progress. Frankenstein's quest grotesquely describes the nature of all rational
ambitions—to factor life into its constituents so that we might
autonomously create and control it. This also aptly describes
the relationship of government to society.

---

*One candidate who frequently used this metaphor was George Wallace,
who, in his campaign for president in 1968, once made the memorable
remark, "they have created a Frankenstein and now their chickens are
coming home to roost."

~ *PART IV* ~
Conclusions

~11~

The Flight from Certainty

A consumer society harnesses the energy of the discontents it produces to enlarge the hegemony of reason in human behavior and the environment. It is founded on the consumer personality, a commonly shared behavioral pattern in which religious needs are translated into material appetites. This behavioral configuration and the culture it serves are the products of an evolutionary conflict between reason and nature which can be traced back to the dawn of hominization. The cultural evolution of the West that preceded the advent of consumer societies has been marked by events which selected in favor of increased flexibility in the uses to which man might put his propositional abilities. However, a close examination of consumer societies shows that the increase in flexibility is misleading. This flexibility, most evident in the entrepreneurial, pioneering, and innovative individuals within a consumer society, ultimately serves to abet the substitution of a confining set of rational controls for religious and natural controls, over behavior and the environment. In the end, entrepreneurial and scientific activity is suffocated by the very forces that produce it. Ironically, the purpose of consumer societies, societies associated with continual change, is the creation of a managed environment safe from change and governed by certainty—the refuge sought 2,400 years ago. It is a goal that can be approached but never attained.

This, in brief, is the argument I have presented. It leaves a host of unanswered questions. My intent has not been to present definitive proof of this radical view of modern behav-

171

ior, but rather to open discussion of an idea about the way consumer societies work. This idea was spurred by my own observation of anomalies that caused me to wonder about our cherished notions of rational autonomy and individual liberty. I believe that the explanation of consumer societies presented accounts for the curious similarities between consumer and voter purchases that first pricked my curiosity. Still, I am not sure that the view presented about the nature of modern societies can ever be more than argued, although I hope that the ideas presented here will spur further investigation. I also hope that my theory of consumer behavior may help adjust our thinking about modern societies to an emerging evolutionary paradigm that is influencing not only the consideration of animal societies, but human societies as well. This brings us to one question which perhaps I should address, although again I do not think it can be answered. This is the question of what will become of consumer societies. Where are we heading?

The emerging evolutionary paradigm I mentioned above offers a clue to the answer. My argument has been that the consumer society—irrational as it may seem to be—is rooted in a belief in rational man that can be traced to Hellenistic times, and a disposition toward nature that can be traced to the dawn of monotheism. As I argued in Chapter Five, both of these paradigms adequately explained the world visible to the inhabitants of the Mediterranean littoral. However, both paradigms have proved inadequate in explaining the world Western man ultimately conquered, a world, for instance, in which man and animals share a common ancestor, and in which the line between what is animal and what is human is becoming increasingly blurred. And so the static, anthropocentric paradigm that saw the birth of science is gradually being supplanted by an evolutionary paradigm deriving from Darwin, who attempted to adjust inconsistencies in the Western vision of reality. The last hundred years have seen the idea of evolution work its way through the various biological and behavioral sciences reshaping the fabric of our vision of reality as it has done so. Such changes in the world of science signal that our perceptions of man's place in nature are changing. These changes cannot help but affect man's posture toward nature, and consequently the moral and philosophical base of the consumer society.

If one force altering man's perception of his role in nature is the discovery that his overarching beliefs are out of accord with reality, another more dramatic force is the realization that his present course will end with one or another type of catastrophe. Such projections of the limits of growth began in modern times with Malthus, the English economist, and in recent years different groups have added nuclear, cancerous, chemical, energy, and climatic eschatologies to the population disaster Malthus forecast. Such alarms are significant whether or not the predictions are fulfilled, for they indicate that a growing segment of the consumer culture sees our future as bankrupt, and despite the popular "I want it now" philosophy, the consumer society is fundamentally dependent on the consumer's belief in the future. The collapse of the myth of progress may temporarily spur consumer self-indulgence, but its long-term effects are an erosion of the belief in materialism and consequently in the consumer, labor, and capitalist bases of society.

Just as there are such broad signals that the myths of a consumer society are losing their hold on our imaginations, there are numerous signals that American culture is projecting various alternatives. Of course, I have stressed throughout this book that a consumer society continually produces alternative cultures and styles which it then harnesses for its own purposes. The only circumstance that lends any credibility to alternatives occurring presently or in the future is the fading luster of the central myths of the consumer society. The question is under what circumstances an alternative will take hold?

In this regard one of the more significant phenomena is the current religious revitalization. Outside the dried husk of the Christian church, numerous neofundamentalist groups have sprung up, related to each other by the intense emotionalism and self-abnegation of their expression of faith. This resurgence recalls the *Bacchae* in which a god long denied creeps back into society by enthralling the young. Many of these groups, such as the Moonies and the Hare Krishna group, seem to undergo a consumer evolution in which their messianic or millenarian fervor is replaced with a hard sell and growth ethic. Moreover a host of quasi-religious groups such as the infamous People's Temple have sprung up, where emotional dependence is centered on an individual rather than Jesus or God. Such groups are millenial movements like the cargo cults we considered earlier, and it is striking that they should be appearing so frequently today. The People's Temple and its appointment in Jonestown merits a brief consideration here, because that causeless martyrdom provides an agon which illuminates how deeply many people wish to escape responsibility and individuality.

Jonestown was an extreme response to primary anxieties of a consumer society: (1) a hunger to believe emotionally in something, and (2) a correlative desire to escape the oppression of rational autonomy and responsibility. In this sense the substrate of Jonestown pervades the various cults that continually spring up in California and elsewhere. Some observers take these properties of cults as indications of a prefascist culture climate simply awaiting a leader whose message is profound enough to speak past the idiosyncrasies that demarcate cult boundaries.

We are at a point of change. The consumer society is fast running out of goodies to offer its members, and with the fading of the dream of the good life, the search is on for a new dream to justify our straitened circumstances or, perhaps, for a leader to point to a villain upon whom we can vent our anger. It is entirely possible that we as a society, like the residents of Jonestown, will choose to go out in a vindicating blaze of glory, rather than face the tarnished, venal reality behind our dreams. Suicide (and what else is nuclear war?) is the ultimate rational act, the ultimate victory of the mind over the body. Nor would it be the first time that a culture chose self-destruction over the admission that it had made a mistake.

One of the functions of religion is to make death tolerable, if not understandable. Jim Jones succeeded all too well at this. His job was made easier by the hollow alternatives offered by society. The material dream is a kind of living death.

Nor should we think that nature has a radical stake in keeping humanity alive. We have been a particularly disorderly creature, and, indeed, have single-handedly brought about the extinction of innumerable creatures with whom we once shared the earth. We flatter ourselves if we think that nature needs mankind. On the contrary, it is on the fact that man finally seems to be realizing his ultimate dependence on nature—in effect a reaffirmation of natural authority—that I base my slim hopes for our survival.

I wrote earlier that the environmental movement poses the most profound threat to the consumer society. At its most radical the environmental movement is pantheistic. This spirit does not see nature as a collection of resources put on earth for man to exploit and consume; rather, it takes an almost primitive perspective on the interrelationship of man and nature. One can see evidence of this spirit in the divisions that mark the way in which different people participate in outdoor sports. The off-road vehicle buffs who are wrecking the southwestern deserts and the snowmobilers who look at forests as a kind of thrill-seeker's Coney Island clearly are filtering their view of nature through consumer eyes. On the other hand, the hikers, climbers, skiers, kyackers, who eschew hyped-up equipment or even trendy backpacker fashions, and who want to put as little as possible between themselves and nature, have an entirely different view of the way to take satisfaction from the wilds. Although they may return to jobs that push them on the merry road to destruction, it is significant that this part of the outdoors "fad" may be the first in the history of the consumer society not to die in a sales boom. This posture toward nature does not require that you buy anything.

There is some irony in the emergence of a way of living that celebrates nonmaterial satisfactions and requires only a minimum of possessions at a time in which material standards of living are being priced out of reach. Are we to end up like the

Hindus who make a virtue of necessity by celebrating poverty? Or, as Bernard Nossiter has proposed, in *Britain, A Future that Works,* are we to end like Britain, adjusting to declining resources through a reemphasis on family and community life?

I do not think that either provides a model for the near future of the consumer society, despite the fact that each projects from trends apparent today in American society. For one thing, Britain might slip comfortably into a woodsy, clubby future, because over the generations she has exported a great proportion of her adventurers and innovators, first through promise of her colonies, now through the rigors of her tax laws. Many of these restless types came here, as have we drawn the more restless and adventurous types from a host of countries. Despite the fact that *our* restless types are now leaving for Alaska, Australia, and other "frontiers," I think that it is still fair to say that American society, compared to the rest of the world, is genetically restless. By accidents of history, we have been bred for change and growth, and that predisposition has not yet had the opportunity to atrophy.

A portion of this entrepreneurial spirit is now devoted to trying to frame an entente between technology and nature through the development of what is called appropriate technology. Just as Western man discovered the inappropriateness of the biblical view of his origins in the jungles of Africa, so have modern technicians discovered the inappropriateness of our technology through their attempts to foist it on the developing countries of Africa and Asia. Alternative technology holds the promise of capturing some form of cheap, nonpolluting energy, and (in the vision of such groups as New Alchemy) virtual self-sufficiency for a family. However, before we applaud the imminent arrival of the New Age, we should remember first that vast supplies of cheap energy got us into the ecological fix we are in now, and that the only real threat to the American economy is self-sufficiency. The power companies in California, ever on the alert for such possibilities, recently tried to encourage the state to tax solar power. Moreover, there is no guarantee that alternative technology might not end up like the counterculture, domesticated within the embrace of the consumer society. We should also remember that devotees of alternative technology cannot signal an immediate shift in the mainstream of society.

Finally, it would be foolish to think that our vast economic combine might be significantly altered without massive dislocations. The Great Depression was really little more than a rhythmic pause in the maturation of the world capitalist economy. A recasting of the fundamental premises of society might occur only after the total collapse of the consumer society. This is not a thrilling prospect for those of us who are simply trying to get by, but it seems to require a fundamental catastrophe in order that society as a whole change its view of the world. Predictions of catastrophe have an unreality until a catastrophe gives a particular Jeremiah some credibility. Constant assurances that California is ripe for a major earthquake have had little effect on the real estate values in the most earthquake-prone parts of the coast. Society needs a dramatic sign that something is wrong with the way it views the world before things begin to change—and such a sign cannot simply be the gradual deterioration of health and happiness, it must be palpable and undeniable like an earthquake or an uncontrollable epidemic.

Even then, erroneous philosophies will not immediately disappear, but will retain their luster as long as their original adherents are still alive. As I tried to show in my discussion of Tahiti, it is not simple for people to abandon a world view, even if they think it is erroneous. The consumer personality is a product of one's upbringing. It will be replaced when those raising children do so with a different set of values, and that might happen only with the destruction of the consumer society.

We live in an overwhelming era. We live amid numerous prophecies of the end of affluence and amid the palpable signs of decay that historians ascribe to the final moments of earlier epochs. Yet, such is the adaptiveness of a consumer society, and such is our belief in its adaptiveness, that we are prevented from acting on these warnings. We are paralyzed by our very freedom. Nothing seems as if it *must* happen, and, as is often pointed out, technological advances have made fools of legions of earlier prophets. Moreover, many people have never lived better. And so, in tandem with the search for meaning, we find a parallel retreat into decadence, self-indulgence, and narcissism. The consumer society continues to roll along despite the diminishing luster of its myths. What this suggests is that we will continue on our present course, and that the probability of one or another of our proposed disasters will rapidly increase until some small event triggers the apocalypse of the consumer society. And that is the moment when the fringe alternatives will have their day. It is impossible to say which alternative will replace the consumer society or when that day will come. One knows only that it becomes more likely with every passing moment.